*The New Black Middle Class*

# The
# New Black
# Middle Class

*Bart Landry*

UNIVERSITY OF CALIFORNIA PRESS
Berkeley   Los Angeles   London

University of California Press
Berkeley and Los Angeles, California

University of California Press, Ltd.
London, England

Copyright © 1987 by The Regents of the University of California

Library of Congress Cataloging in Publication Data

Landry, Bart.
  The new Black middle class.

    1. Afro-Americans—Social conditions—1975–    .  2. Middle
classes—United States.    3. United States—Race relations.
I. Title.
E185.86.L35    1987        305.8'96073        86–24975
ISBN 0–520–05942–5 (alk. paper)


Printed in the United States of America


1 2 3 4 5 6 7 8 9

*For my parents,
Joseph and Bernadette Landry,
and for Ayo*

# Contents

# Preface

My interest in the black middle class goes back to 1973 when research on the general economic condition of all blacks made me aware of how few black families fell into the middle-income category. Those families who did almost invariably had two earners. A thorough search of scholarly and popular literature revealed an immense gap in our knowledge of this group of blacks. The bulk of the literature examined the condition of poor blacks, particularly those living in the ghettos of our inner cities, leaving the impression that all blacks were poor. Occasionally, an article in a popular magazine revealed the existence of a group of economically secure blacks in some major city. Sometimes these blacks were referred to as "middle class" or even as an "aristocracy." But social scientists were almost completely silent about the size of this group, their origins, and their living conditions.

The notable exception to this trend was E. Franklin Frazier's study of the black middle class, first published in French in 1955 under the title *Bourgeoisie Noire* and then released to the American public in translation as the *Black Bourgeoisie* in 1957. Controversial in its day, Frazier's work has continued to stimulate intermittent discussion about the accuracy of his scathing criticism of middle-class blacks in the 1950s. Accurate or not, the criticism that Frazier's study did not rest on systematic and representative empirical data remains true. The often-heated discussion, however, generated few empirical studies of the black middle class in ensuing decades. In fact, in 1976, when the data for this study were collected, no analysis of the black middle class based on national representative data had yet appeared—a condition that unfortunately remains true today.

My search of the literature uncovered another disturbing fact. There could be found no consensus in either scholarly or popular literature on the definition of middle class. Some writers defined the group by their educational level, others by their income, and still others by their occupations or some combination of these characteristics. Again, I was forced into a frustrating search of the literature of the meaning of class. Here, too, I found no consensus. In the end I was forced to take a position with which I felt comfortable, given existing theoretical discussions and empirical findings. In taking this position, I do not mean to imply that it is the only one possible or even the best one. I do believe, however, that it is clear and defensible.

This study is not viewed as the last word on the subject. Rather, it is hoped that it will stimulate more research on the black middle class, both on issues covered and on many that were omitted or only briefly touched on. Such research would lead to greater understanding of the diversity existing within the black community.

A study such as this could not have been carried out without assistance. I wish to express my thanks especially to the Twentieth Century Fund for its generous financial support, which made possible the collection of a national survey on which the bulk of this study is based. In addition, the Computer Science Center at the

University of Maryland provided valuable computer time for my analysis of the survey. Audits and Surveys, under the direction of Lloyd Kirban, gave me welcome technical advice while I was completing the survey instrument and did an excellent job in collecting the data. I am also grateful for support provided by the Wilson Center in Washington, D.C., where part of the writing was done. During the course of this study I benefited from conversation with or comments on parts of the manuscript from Andrew Billingsley, James E. Blackwell, Jan E. Dizard, Maurice Garnier, Al-Tony Gilmore, Jerald Hage, Charles Hamilton, Ruth Hamilton, Sharon Harley, Robert B. Hill, Cora B. Marrett, Robert Perrucci, George Ritzer, John Scanzoni, David Segal, and William J. Wilson. Equally important was the assistance I received from a number of graduate students who helped me with processing the data and doing computer runs. My appreciation is extended to Tom Patterson, Margaret Platt Jendrek, and Mike Massagli. The skilled editorial comments of Lynn Moore and Sheila Berg helped make this a more readable work. Much of the typing was done by Karen Flowers and Gerry Todd, assisted by Melissa Kelly, Terri Kieckhefer, and Bernadette Lasobik.

University of Maryland                      Bart Landry
College Park, Maryland
September 1986

# Introduction:
# Middle-Class Blacks and
# the American Dream

Progress remained an elusive goal for all but a few blacks in America for almost a century following emancipation. In a country where progress is measured by movement up the class ladder, blacks found themselves trapped on the ladder's lower rungs. During the nineteenth century, first as slaves and then as freedmen, black workers formed the backbone of the southern agricultural economy but were denied a role in the industrializing North. The millions of jobs being created in the automobile factories, the steel and textile mills, the mines, and the slaughterhouses went to white immigrants from Europe who came to America seeking a better life. The plight of black workers throughout the North was poignantly expressed in the lament of a Detroit whitewasher in 1891:

> First it was de Irish, den it was de Dutch, and now it's de Polacks as grinds us down. I s'pose when dey (the Poles) gets like de Irish and stands up for a fair price, some odder strangers'll come over de sea 'nd jine de faimily and cut us down again.[1]

Only after passage of a restrictive immigration bill in 1924 and the First World War combined to shut off

1

immigration from Europe did black workers get an opportunity to move into the industrial economy of the North in meaningful numbers. Opportunity, however grudgingly afforded, was at last knocking at the doors of blacks. And they responded enthusiastically, migrating in the millions to the industrial centers of the North. Had it not been for their willingness to do so, American industry would certainly have suffered a serious setback.

While this chance to enter America's industrial economy represented significant progress for blacks, they nevertheless found themselves displaced by white workers whenever possible and barred from the skilled trades. Blacks also found they were denied the opportunity to join the white middle class in supplying the brain power and intellectual skills of the nation as scientists, researchers, academicians, writers, and even as clerical workers. About the only middle-class occupations accessible to blacks were those that served the needs of the black community—they could be teachers, ministers, social workers, and, occasionally, doctors and lawyers. George Washington Carver, W. E. B. Du Bois, Ralph Bunche, Thurgood Marshall, and others who made important contributions had to do so against tremendous odds. These black men, however, signaled that many thousands more were waiting to make their contributions to the life of the nation but could not do so because of discrimination. Such restrictions severely limited the upward mobility of blacks so that at midcentury only 10 percent of all black workers held middle-class jobs compared to 40 percent of white workers.

Once again, a national upheaval was required to enable blacks to climb to the next rung of the ladder. First it was the Civil War, followed by a major restrictive immigration bill and two world wars; now it was the civil rights movement and a booming economy in the 1960s. As a result of these last two events, the black middle class doubled in size during the 1960s, encompassing 27 percent of all black workers by 1970. Though blacks still lacked an upper class, they finally had a middle class freed from the past legal strictures of discrimination and found for the first time a wide variety of occupations opened to them.

For these reasons, I call the black middle class of the 1960s a *new* black middle class. Its emergence marked a major turning point in the life of black people in the United States. New opportunities at this level of the class structure gave renewed hope to the aspirations of working-class black parents. No longer were the doors of many colleges and universities closed to them. And a college degree need not automatically mean preparation for a career teaching black children or as a social worker in the black community. Now there was the chance that their sons and daughters could also aspire to become accountants, lawyers, engineers, scientists, and architects. This was a significant development both for the nation and for the black community itself. For the former, it meant a broadening of the pool of talent from which to draw for its development; for the latter, it represented fuller participation in society and more leadership and economic resources.

What life is like for this new black middle class and what the future holds is the subject of this work. The first chapter traces the historical events leading up to this point, from a small mulatto elite in postemancipation decades, through an old black middle class in the first half of the twentieth century to the new black middle class in the 1960s. Chapter 2 analyzes the dynamics of events in the 1960s that created favorable conditions for the emergence of the new black middle class. In addition, the new black middle class is compared to the old, and the question of the significance of race—a topic frequently returned to in subsequent chapters—is taken up. Chapter 3 examines the mobility experiences of middle-class blacks and whites, the paths followed by each, and the effort required to reach the middle class. Chapter 4 compares the occupational and financial achievements of blacks and whites who have reached the middle class so as to understand the degree to which middle-class blacks have attained parity with whites—or still fall short. In chapters 5 and 6, the standards of living of middle-class blacks and whites are analyzed in depth, including an assessment of the extent to which black and white families depend on the economic contribution of wives, the amount and sources of middle-class wealth, and the quantity and quality of material goods possessed. The life style of the new black middle class will be the subject of chapter 7, with comparisons made between the old and new black middle classes as well as between middle-class blacks and whites. Chapter 8 examines the effects of the changed economic conditions of the 1970s and 1980s on the new black middle class to discover how it fared in this period of recessions, high inflation, and high unemployment. I will also attempt to forecast the prospects of the black middle class from an analysis of societal trends and forces affecting its growth and economic position.

It is an irony of history that at the point when blacks developed a viable middle class, economic conditions that had been transforming the United States into a middle-class society and had promised unlimited growth changed abruptly. So profound are these changes in the 1970s and 1980s that it now appears it is a tarnished dream to which the black middle class has awakened. The results of this study should provide a comprehensive picture of the new black middle class that emerged during the 1960s as compared to its white counterpart and some clues to what lies ahead in the rest of this decade and even into the 1990s. In doing so, it should also contribute importantly to the debate over the significance of race for the black middle class and provide some insight into the respective roles of class and race in the United States today.

## DEFINING THE BLACK MIDDLE CLASS

Two of the most frequent questions that arise about my research are, "How do you define class?" and "How do you define middle class?" Most laymen and not a few scholars tend to define class in terms of income; some scholars include education in the definition. While it is difficult to resist placing greatest importance on income, there are no sound criteria for establishing class boundaries defined by it. Is the lower boundary the population's median income? Is it $20,000 or $30,000? What is the upper boundary, $50,000 or $60,000? How is one to decide? And how much education qualifies one for the middle class—an undergraduate degree? What about those who have completed two or three years of college? Are they middle class? As I will explain below, from a Weberian point of view, education is a *cause* or *source* of an individual's class position rather than a defining characteristic, and income is *one* of the many rewards resulting from one's class position. Neither income nor education, therefore, are part of the definition of class.

From a Marxian perspective, classes are bonded, categorical groups whose identity derives from their different relationships to the means of production. In other words, the meaning of class revolves around the ownership and use of capital. In his scheme, Marx tended to contrast those who owned the means of production (large corporations and banks) with those who made a living by working for these owners. This is not a distinction between "haves and have-nots" but a more fundamental one between those who hire and those who are hired. Marx called the owners of large businesses the bourgeoisie. Today we are more likely to refer to them as the "upper class." However, Marx called those entrepreneurs who owned small businesses, hiring only a few workers or none at all, the petite bourgeoisie and predicted that they would eventually be forced out of business by large corporations. This was, of course, before the existence of antitrust laws and small business loans. But even today, the difficulty small enterprises have competing and surviving in a corporate economy is well known.

With a few exceptions, Marx classified all those who were nonowners as "workers." Whether unskilled, skilled, or educated, those who depended on others to hire them were workers. While we must admit this argument possesses a certain cogency, we feel some reluctance in placing all workers in the same amorphous class. There must be some difference between an engineer and a taxicab driver. It is here that the ideas of Max Weber, one of Marx's chief critics, prove useful.

While recognizing the basic class division between those who hire and those who are hired, Weber also allowed for class distinctions among the hired, the propertyless. These distinctions result from the different levels of education and skill workers bring to trade for positions (occupations) in the marketplace. The more education and skills, the better the position secured. Historically, those individuals with more education have been able to enter occupations that bring greater economic rewards in terms of income, mobility, fringe benefits, and stability as well as more intangible rewards such as degree of control over one's work situation, independence, and prestige.

In time, this approach led to the recognition of a major class cleavage between nonmanual and manual workers, or—to use the more modern terminology—between white-collar and blue-collar workers. As the number of nonmanual workers increased during the latter stage of Western industrialization, another term came into use: "middle class." Poised between the owners of corporations and banks and manual workers, nonmanual workers came to be viewed as relatively well-off in the class structure. Compared to blue-collar workers, they did clean work, did not punch a clock, enjoyed greater prestige, and, especially, earned higher incomes and received better fringe benefits. Resulting differences in life chances and life styles were striking.

White-collar workers historically have included five occupational groups: (1) professionals, (2) managers (nonowners), (3) sales workers, (4) clerical workers, and (5) small businessmen.[2] Each group has its own history as well as a distinct position and role in the class structure. Within industrial societies, entrepreneurs have played the major catalytic role in developing the economy, with the most successful becoming owners of the means of production (large corporations and banks) in the classical Marxian sense and forming an upper class. The thousands of small businessmen who are neither part of the upper class nor salaried workers occupy an ambiguous position. The tendency has been to see them as a separate class positioned between the upper class and all salaried and wage workers or as part of a middle class. I take the position that they are part of the middle class.

Studies have shown that all ethnic groups in the United States have produced a stratum of small entrepreneurs whose principal market—at least initially—was composed of members of their own group. Eventually, many small businesses, such as Chinese laundries and restaurants, succeeded in enlarging their markets and appealing to a more general population. It is in terms of this phenomenon that I will evaluate attempts by blacks to enter the world of business and measure their success. While blacks became entrepreneurs as early as before emancipation, I am interested in them as an important stratum of an emerging black middle class in the twentieth century.

Like entrepreneurs, professionals also have a long history, at least as represented by a segment of that group, that is, doctors and lawyers. They too had an ambiguous position in the class structure during the early development of Western capitalism. Marx was inclined to see at least some professionals, particularly lawyers, as part of the upper class since they often worked in the service of that class. In time, professionals in other occupations, such as engineers, scientists, teachers, and social workers, began to grow in number and in importance. Though the early professionals were usually self-employed, these new professionals, and increasingly, many doctors and lawyers, worked for fixed salaries. While Marxians may yet debate their position in the class structure, Weber and subsequent scholars would place them in the middle class, which is the approach I take here. It will become clear in the course of this study that the entrance of blacks into professional occupations during the first half of the twentieth century was entirely a factor of the black community's need for certain basic services such as health care, religion, education, and, to a more limited extent, legal aid. When direct service to the black community was not involved, blacks were usually barred from entering a professional field, thus distorting their role in the class structure.

Managerial, clerical, and sales jobs were the latest white-collar occupations to appear in industrial societies; in Marx's day, such positions were few. Their appearance and growth in number paralleled a later stage of industrialization, as capitalism shifted more and more to medium-size and large firms and corporations. As this movement progressed, there was an increasing need for owners of growing businesses to hire managers to help with the day-to-day operations. At the same time, a growing number of clerical positions were created to assist owners and managers, and retail outlets grew from "mom and pop" stores to department stores requiring larger sales staffs. The class position of managers has been a subject of considerable debate recently, with some scholars arguing that they constitute a separate class, others locating them in the upper class of owners, and still others seeing them as members of the middle class.[3] The class position of clerical and sales workers is also being debated, even among Weberians, but the tendency has been to see this group also as a stratum within the middle class—although the least prosperous of all.

At the heart of this latter debate are changes in the economy generally and in the working conditions of clerical workers particularly. On the one hand, there were those who began arguing in the 1950s that the rapid rise in postwar living standards was placing formerly luxury consumer goods in the homes of manual workers and transforming the country into a middle-class nation (a point to which I return in chap. 2).[4] On the other hand, some have argued that the deskilling of clerical work through office automation is transforming such work into manual labor. There is no doubt that clerical workers no longer resemble the once important and powerful office clerk. It should not be forgotten, however, that as recently as forty or fifty years ago, clerical and sales work represented significant upward mobility from the drudgery of manual labor. In the United States, it was work reserved for native-born whites and was not penetrated by immigrants to any significant degree until the second and third generations. Blacks found themselves completely shut out of these jobs until the 1960s.

Though clerical and sales work has become increasingly fragmented and feminized today, there remain a great variety of positions, including highly paid executive secretaries and secretaries in small businesses who often perform managerial tasks. Often overlooked in this debate is the fact that male clerical and sales workers frequently occupy the higher paid positions. In sales, they are most often found in the more lucrative areas of durable goods and furniture or as representatives for industrial and pharmaceutical products; among clerical workers, they are often in supervisory positions. These males earn salaries comparable to or higher than those of skilled manual workers, and they have the added advantage of potential mobility into management careers. Skilled blue-collar workers earn high wages but cannot penetrate the ranks of management beyond the position of foreman.

While some clerical and sales jobs held by women have experienced deskilling and a corresponding weakening of their economic position, it is not at all clear that clerical and sales occupations *taken as a group* are economically weaker than those of skilled blue-collar workers. Most research comparing blue-collar workers with clerical workers has concluded that the manual/nonmanual dichotomy is still valid.[5] And there is to date relatively little research on the economic position of female clerical and sales workers.[6] In this study, then, I follow the traditional Weberian position, which includes clerical and sales workers in the middle class. Frequently, however, the analysis will be reported separately for the professional-managerial stratum and the sales-clerical stratum, often referred to as upper middle class and lower middle class, respectively. The professional-managerial stratum includes professionals, managers, and small businessmen; the sales-clerical stratum is made up of all sales and clerical positions plus firemen and policemen.

To summarize my position on the composition of the middle class, I include all white-collar workers and small businessmen plus a number of service occupations that I consider on a par with sales and clerical work, such as firemen, policemen, and dental assistants. These service occupations require a period of training before admission and may even attempt to maintain professional standards. Of these latter occupations, however, only policemen and firemen appear in my sample. This minor reclassification is not meant to be exhaustive. The problem with reclassification of occupations is that so many positions with the same job title vary tremendously in responsibilities, wages, and working conditions. Secretaries range from those in mechanized typing pools to prestigious and sometimes powerful assistants to top corporate executives. "Clerical worker" includes those requiring only knowledge of the alphabet to perform their duties as file clerks as well as a variety of postal clerks and those with statistical training. Any list of occupations included in the middle or working class, or strata of these classes, will inevitably have limitations. However, the concept of class does not rest so much on the development of an infallible list of occupations for each class as on the existence of overall, gross differences in the real economic rewards received by individuals in different occupational groups.

## THE WORKING CLASS AND THE UNDERCLASS

To the extent that the working class is touched upon in this study, it too is divided into two strata. One stratum, which includes skilled and semiskilled workers, is referred to by the shortened form, "skilled working class"; the other, which includes unskilled workers, is referred to as "unskilled working class." I prefer "unskilled working class" to "lower class" because of the pejorative status connotation of the latter term. "Upper working class" and "lower working class" were also considered.

The advantage of the term "unskilled working class" is its explicit designation of the group of workers in whom I am most interested and among whom blacks are disproportionately concentrated. These include laborers such as construction workers, garbage collectors, and longshoremen as well as domestic workers and many in the hotel and restaurant industries. These jobs require such low-level skills that they can be learned in a few weeks. They are the most disposable of all workers, many earning minimum wage except in cases where they are unionized.

As will become clear in this study, it is as much the overconcentration of black workers in the unskilled working class as the slow growth of the black middle class that has distinguished the black class structure from that of whites. While the white unskilled working class declined steadily as the white middle class grew, the black unskilled working class remained the single largest group of black workers until about 1978. As late as 1986, it still represented over 25 percent of all black workers compared to 17 percent of all white workers. By 1990, the unskilled working class is still likely to contain one-fourth of all black workers. Any study of the black middle class would do well, therefore, to at least make a passing acknowledgment of this fact for the sake of perspective.

There is yet another group within the class structure that has received increased attention from both scholars and the press: the underclass. Most similar conceptually to Marx's *lumpenproletariat*, the underclass includes those without steady employment, unskilled day workers, the long-term unemployed, discouraged workers who have dropped out of the labor force, unemployed youth who have dropped out of school, individuals on permanent welfare, and those living off illegal activities such as prostitution and drugs. This "fallout" group is an important one within the class structure as it repre sents those who have failed to get a foothold even at the level of the unskilled working class. They deserve the attention accorded them today because of their significance for the entire class system in the United States and the overconcentration of blacks among them. They are not discussed in this study, however, except in passing and do not appear in the statistical analysis. "Poor" includes most of the underclass as well as much of the unskilled working class. Although a popular concept, it lacks sufficient precision from a class perspective and will not often appear in these pages.

One other decision taken in this study which is related to definition should be clarified. In the past, researchers have assigned to families the class position of husbands under the assumption that a family's class position is determined by the husband as principal breadwinner. With the increased involvement of females (both married and single) in the labor force, it is difficult to see how this practice can be justified today. In 1980, 58.9 percent of black women with husbands present and 49.9 percent of white women with husbands present were in the labor force, a large proportion of them full-time. In view of this, there is a need for a measure of class position that is a function of the combined class positions of husbands and wives rather than of husbands alone. After some experimentation, the approach taken here was to assign a family the class position of the spouse with the *highest* individual class, provided he or she was a full-time worker. This means that a family in which the husband worked as a salesman and the wife as an elementary schoolteacher was classified by the wife's occupation—upper middle class—instead of the husband's—lower middle class. Likewise, if the wife worked as a nurse and the husband as an assembly line worker, the family was considered middle class rather than working class. There was one exception to this rule: in cases where the husband was a skilled worker and the wife was in a clerical or sales occupation, the family was classified as skilled (therefore, working class) because of the assumed superior market position of skilled males over many female clerical or sales workers.

The implications of this approach to family class are significant. In a group such as blacks in which females have had greater access historically to white-collar occupations and have been employed full-time at higher rates than in other groups, women contribute relatively more to the economic well-being of the family. When translated into a class dimension, as in this study, it becomes apparent that the class position of black families is more frequently determined by wives than is the case in white families, a point I will touch on in chapter 5.

## DATA USED

Several types of data were used in this study. The first chapter draws on E. Franklin Frazier's works and other case studies of black communities in the late nineteenth and early twentieth century to piece together the early history of the black mulatto elite and the old black middle class up to 1960. Most of this book focuses on a detailed analysis of the *new* black middle class in the mid-1970s based on a national representative survey. Face-to-face interviews were conducted with both middle-class blacks and middle-class whites in twenty-one Standard Metropolitan Statistical Areas (SMSAs) of the northeastern, north-central, and southern regions of the United States in spring 1976. The West was excluded because the additional cost could not be justified given the small proportion of the black population residing there. The sampling design followed the standard multistage probability type, with units to be included at the

SMSA level selected proportional to the distribution of middle-income blacks ($8,000 or more in 1976) within SMSAs (of each region) having populations of ten thousand or more. To maximize comparability, the sample of whites was selected from the same SMSAs as that of blacks; however, within SMSAs, the white and black samples were drawn proportional to the unique distribution of each. Blacks were selected randomly within census tracts and quotas filled at the household level with callbacks. Respondents were selected in such a way as to yield roughly an equal division of females and males. To ensure a high proportion of middle-class black and white households in the final sample, households were screened, and only those were interviewed which had both spouses present, had family incomes of $12,000 or above in 1976 (in 1986, equivalent to $23,008), and where the respondent was less than 65 years old. The final tally of usable interviews was 556 blacks and 600 whites.

To obtain information on the neighborhood environment of the black and white middle classes, housing, education, income, and occupational characteristics of each census tract sampled were computerized and appended to the record of each respondent. This information was used in the discussion of the life style of the black middle class (chap. 6).

The fourth data source is census data from the 1970s and 1980s (used extensively in chap. 8). Much of these data were drawn from unpublished tables supplied to me by the Census Bureau and the Bureau of Labor Statistics and represent the most up-to-date information available on occupation and income.

Some limitations of the data, particularly the survey data, should be pointed out. The decision to include only households in which both spouses were present was made to ensure the greatest number of usable cases possible. Had single-parent families been included, there may not have been a sufficient number of such families in the final sample to allow subanalysis of these households having lower incomes than those in which both spouses were present. This decision, however, has the drawback of excluding a significant group of middle-class families, especially among blacks. While the proportion of single-parent families is far lower among middle-class blacks than among other classes, a rising divorce rate has resulted in a growing number of single-parent middle-class families in the 1980s. The effect of their omission from the major part of this study is that the economic strength of the black middle class taken as a whole is *overstated*. This becomes clear in chapter 8, where census data for all middle-class families with a full-time, year-round employed head are used. Since these data include single-parent families, we find that the average income of this group of middle-class families in 1976 was about $3,300 lower than that of my sample of two-parent families. Single-parent families are smaller by definition, however; hence their lower average income frequently does not represent a lower living standard, especially for those in the upper middle class.

The decision by the Census Bureau to introduce a new occupational classification in 1980 raised another kind of problem. While there has always been some occupational reclassification between decennial censuses, these have never been significant enough to prevent meaningful comparisons with previous censuses. But the 1980 occupational reclassification is so radical a change that most comparisons with previous surveys cannot be made. Through careful analysis of the 1980 and 1970 occupational classifications, it was possible to carry forward comparisons for the total middle class to 1983. Most detailed analysis, however, could not be extended beyond 1981, the last year for which the Census Bureau published data using the 1970 occupational classification.

Finally, there are many who will feel some frustration when reading dollar figures for 1976 (the year of the survey) and will want to know the equivalent for more recent years. In chapter 8, I sometimes give the 1986 equivalent of 1976 dollars. Between 1976 and 1986, the cost-of-living index almost doubled. To obtain 1986 equivalents for 1976 dollars, therefore, it is safe to simply double the 1976 figure. (The actual increase is 1.934.) By multiplying this ratio by 1976 dollars, one can obtain the exact 1986 equivalent. The equivalent for other years can be obtained by dividing the cost-of-living index for the year in question by the index for 1976 (115.2) and using the resulting ratio as the multiplier for 1976 dollars.

# 1

# The Old Black Middle Class: Dilemma of Race in a Class Society

It would be difficult to find three more solid representatives of the old black middle class than Booker T. Washington, C. C. Spaulding, and James Weldon Johnson. Washington, pioneering educator, president of Tuskegee Institute, organizer of the Negro Business League, and recognized leader of the black community, won national and international recognition for his speech at the Atlanta Exposition in 1895. Spaulding, a black businessman, could boast of founding the largest and most successful black insurance company in the United States—the North Carolina Mutual Life Insurance Company. And Johnson, a poet, novelist, and songwriter, was also a diplomat and leader of the National Association for the Advancement of Colored People (NAACP). Had they been white, these three men would have lived the sheltered existence of the upper middle class, untouched by the petty annoyances that are the common experiences of the poor. But being black, all three suffered the violence and indignities that dogged the heels of all blacks in the early decades of this century.

Washington was twice attacked and beaten by whites, the first time only hours after his famous speech at the

18

Atlanta Exposition: on a train bound for Massachusetts, an irate conductor beat him for refusing to turn his seat around.[1] Some years later, in 1911, while attempting to locate the auditor of Tuskegee Institute in New York City, Washington was again attacked, this time by "a big German" who accused him of hanging around a building. Washington ran into the streets, was attacked by other whites who joined his first assailant, and was saved from severe injury only by the chance presence of a detective and a policeman.[2] In 1919, when the NAACP held its annual convention in Cleveland and the talk was of the liberal climate of that city and its abolitionist tradition, Johnson—then field secretary for the NAACP—was refused service in a downtown restaurant because he was black.[3] Some years later, in 1931, Spaulding was severely beaten by a white soda jerk in Durham, North Carolina, for daring to sip a coke across the color line.[4] Ironically, the soda fountain from which he was ejected was housed in a building secretly owned by Spaulding himself.

These incidents, occurring in both the North and the South, emphasize the essential dilemma of the then-emerging old black middle class: no amount of fame or success could shield any black against the fundamental and all-pervasive subordination forced on blacks of all backgrounds and occupations at that time. That a black middle class developed at all was itself a fluke, an accident running counter to the historical norms and trends of American society, which attempted to restrict all blacks to the unskilled working class.

As recently as 1910, 50 percent of all blacks were part of a rural proletariat of sharecroppers and subsistence farmers, while another 39 percent were concentrated among unskilled laborers and service workers. This pattern held wherever black people lived in the United States but especially in the South, where almost 90 percent of blacks resided. Only 3 percent of all black workers in 1910 held white-collar positions, compared to 24 percent of whites, and only 2.5 percent were in skilled blue-collar jobs (fig. 1). Had a restrictive immigration bill and two world wars not cut off the supply of white immigrant labor from Europe, blacks would not have entered the industrial sector of the economy in any meaningful capacity for at least decades to come.

In the one hundred years between 1820 and 1920, the period during which the United States became an industrial society, almost thirty million European immigrants arrived to fill the country's insatiable demand for labor. Between 1901 and 1920 alone, over twelve million Europeans immigrated to the United States. Throughout this one-hundred-year period, blacks in the North and the South found themselves largely passed over in preference for white immigrant workers.

The 1924 National Origins Quota Act—a highly discriminatory bill aimed at restricting Eastern and Southern European immigrants—changed this situation dramatically. By limiting total annual immigration to 150,000 and assigning the largest quotas to Western Europeans, who were now disinclined to emigrate, the flow of European immigrants came to a virtual halt. Only then did white northern industrialists, who previously had demonstrated a preference for white immigrant labor over the abundant supply of southern black workers, turn in desperation to recruiting blacks for their factories, stockyards, and steel mills. Blacks responded eagerly to this opportunity—4.6 million between 1910 and 1960—in their desire to escape the oppression of the South and their subordinate status.

The first wave of this black migration headed toward the industrial cities of the North. By 1920, Chicago, Detroit, New York, Cleveland, Cincinnati, Columbus, Philadelphia, and Pittsburgh contained almost 40 percent of the North's black population. In some cases, the volume of migrants was staggering. Chicago received

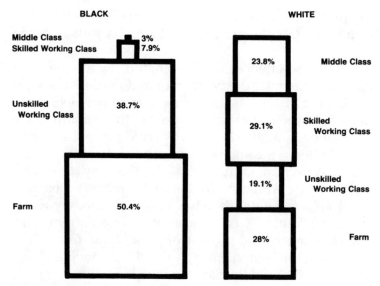

Fig. 1. Black and white class structures in 1910.

some fifty thousand black migrants during an eighteen-month period in 1917 and 1918.[5] Detroit's black population increased 611.3 percent during the 1910s; Cleveland and Chicago followed with increases of 307.8 and 148.2 percent, respectively.[6]

The poverty, disillusionment, and misery blacks suffered in the industrial North has often been documented. But another, brighter side of that picture is usually overlooked. These burgeoning black urban communities provided an opportunity for the emergence of a black middle class of teachers, doctors, dentists, undertakers, realtors, insurance agents, ministers, newspaper editors, and small businessmen who attempted to meet the needs of a black community that whites were often unwilling to serve. Their emergence was a long and difficult process that began with a small mulatto elite at the top of the black social pyramid in postemancipation years and ended with the development of a black class structure in the early decades of the twentieth century which was topped by a small but significant middle class, in the North as well as in the South.

As the experiences of Washington, Spaulding, and Johnson illustrate, the position of middle-class blacks in the United States has been unique from the beginning. Because of their status as members of the minority black population, middle-class blacks have not been able to seek shelter in the anonymity and security of the broad-based American middle class in the way upwardly mobile white ethnics have. Instead, whatever their personal achievements, they have been plagued by a certain marginality. It is because of their unique history and experiences and because of present differences that we are justified in speaking of a "black middle class" and a "white middle class" rather than simply of the American middle class. Were this not the case, there would be no reason for a study of the black middle class, since their story would be inseparable from that of middle-class whites.

Besides the need to gain a better understanding of this group within the black population, there is another reason for studying the black middle class: it serves as a bellwether of blacks and their progress in the United States. Upward mobility has always been considered a hallmark of life in the United States, at once a unique American ideology and a driving force behind individual motivation. It is an aspiration embedded in the lore of our society in such expressions as "rags to riches" and "office boy to company president." While millions of white ethnics have experienced the reality of this aspiration as successful small businessmen and professionals, there is a real question about the extent to which blacks have experienced similar successes. Recently, an argument was made by William Wilson for the declining significance of race, especially with respect to the experiences of middle-class blacks.[7] It is a thesis that has been

praised by some and condemned by many more, especially by black intellectuals who see in this statement a
dangerous misrepresentation of the contemporary black
experience.

The question remains: Have middle-class blacks, like
their white counterparts, finally "made it," or do they
remain marginal, second-class Americans even at the
height of their personal achievements? It is in pursuit
of an answer to this important question that this study
has been undertaken. To the extent that middle-class
blacks reach parity with their white counterparts there
is hope and inspiration for those still below that level;
to the extent that middle-class blacks remain unequal
the hope is dampened and the need more urgent to
make the dream a reality. In this chapter, I examine the
first two phases in the development of the black middle
class: (1) the period of the old mulatto elite, from emancipation to 1915, and (2) the period during which the
old black middle class emerged, from 1915 to 1960. The
remaining chapters are devoted to the third phase, that
of the new black middle class, from around 1960 and
continuing to the present.

## NEITHER WHITE NOR BLACK:
## THE OLD MULATTO ELITE

After the upheavals of the Civil War and emancipation
subsided and free black communities began to be established, internal differences soon emerged. Frazier argued that some of these differences were rooted in
distinctions found in preemancipation plantation slave
communities and among blacks free before the Civil
War, not the least of which was a distinction in skin
color.[8] Whatever the merits of this argument, the group
that rose to the top in the emerging black communities
everywhere did consist primarily of mulattoes. This pre-

dominance of individuals of light complexion at the top of the black community structure from the very beginning bears some explanation, especially given the important role color has historically played among blacks.

There is no doubt that before emancipation, mulattoes already formed a significant group among free blacks but not among the slave population. By 1850, more than one out of every three free blacks was a mulatto, compared to less than one of ten slaves. In some states, mulattoes clearly predominated among free blacks; for instance, in Louisiana, 15,000 of the 18,000 free blacks were mulattoes, and they also predominated in Virginia and Mississippi. These mulattoes, primarily the offspring of slave women and white masters, had been freed because of kinship to their owners. This kinship had often brought certain advantages during slavery, such as the opportunity to learn a trade or even to learn to read. Once free, former slaves were sometimes able to translate this early advantage into a more lucrative and higher-status occupation—as a skilled artisan, a domestic servant for a wealthy white family, or even a self-employed businessman catering to the needs of a wealthy white clientele. Barbering, especially, became an important occupation for blacks beginning around the 1840s when the style of men's hair changed from long to short, requiring frequent clipping. The skill could be learned in about a year, and in time, an ambitious individual could own his own shop. In Philadelphia, black caterers, many having the city's wealthiest whites as clients, were numerous enough to form a guild around 1840.[9] Many free blacks were also successful in acquiring some education. This was especially true in northern and border cities such as Boston, Baltimore, Washington, D.C., Philadelphia, and New York. But even in southern states with prohibitions against the education of blacks, many of those in urban areas were able to learn to read and write and even to gain a formal education.

The distinction of white ancestry among a despised and powerless group and opportunities to capitalize on this characteristic for economic and social gain led to the emergence of a small mulatto elite in urban communities in both the North and South. Feeling superior to the unmixed Negroes around them, they held themselves apart and developed their own social and community life—often patterned after the life style of whites whom they were able to observe closely because of their frequent contacts in service capacities. The clearly defined status group of mulattoes that had appeared by the time of the Civil War rose to the top of the social pyramid in black communities and continued to grow during the fifty years after emancipation. Eventually, they were to be overtaken by events stirring in society, to be replaced by a group of black entrepreneurs and professionals rooted in and serving the black community itself.

STATUS VERSUS CLASS

I have referred to this early mulatto elite as a *status* group to emphasize that a true middle class had not yet appeared within the black community. The distinction between status groups and classes is an important one, one that is far too often confused or overlooked. Status groups emerge out of the *subjective evaluation* of community members; classes are based on *objective positions* within the economic system. This distinction, first made by Max Weber in his critique of Marx, does not deny the basic Marxian dichotomy between those who own and exploit investment capital (property) for profit and those who depend on salaries or wages for their livelihood. Rather, Weber went beyond dividing the world into the propertied versus the propertyless, recognizing further class distinctions among the propertyless salaried workers and wage earners themselves. In addition, he pointed to a second mechanism of social ranking—status.

The prototype for status groups in Weber's time was the landed gentry, for whom family background was as important as economic means and a necessary criterion for membership in the group. Members not only belonged to old families but restricted themselves to marrying within this group, socialized only with other members, and strove to maintain similar life styles. In the United States, though status groups have always had less importance than in Europe, we can think of the Blue Books in some older cities such as Boston and such upper-class clubs as the Links and the Century Association in New York, the Duquesne Club in Pittsburgh, and the Chicago Club in Chicago. The subjectivity of status groups lies in the *criteria* used to determine membership eligibility. Unlike the objective economic characteristics of classes, status attributes emerge out of the values of group members and thus vary from place to place and from group to group as well as over time. Family background, address, membership in social clubs and churches, consumption patterns, education, and skin color are just some of the most common traits used by status groups to set boundaries, but the number of status characteristics is theoretically endless.

In the United States, the most elaborate mapping of the status system of a community can be found in W. Lloyd Warner's exhaustive study of a small New England town, which he called Yankee City, in the 1940s.[10] The later application of Warner's approach by a number of his students to black communities in Natchez, Mississippi, in the 1930s and Chicago in the 1940s provided considerable insights into differences in the status structures of black and white communities in other parts of the country.[11] Unfortunately, Warner and his students often used the terms "class" and "status" interchangeably, leading to a blurring of the distinction between status groups and classes. A careful reading of Warner's work reveals, however, that his definition of the groups studied parallels very closely Weber's definition of status groups.[12]

The subjectivity of the process through which status groups emerge and are ranked makes it inevitable that every community will have a full range of status groups, from high to low. The process is similar to the jockeying for position that takes place in a gang, social club, school, or almost any group that maintains a prolonged association. Gradually, some members emerge as acknowledged leaders, as more respected or less respected, and eventually an informal ranking of most members from lowest to highest occurs based on criteria unique to the group. At this level, it may be daring, athletic ability, or the giving of lavish parties that determines who holds the position at the top. In the larger society, those individuals with the most desirable characteristics in a community will be ranked highest, and if numerous enough, they will form a group. Those with the least desirable characteristics will be ranked lowest, and the remainder will fall in between.

It is otherwise with the process of class formation. Whether we follow Marx and think of classes in terms of relationships to the means of production, thus emphasizing the distinction between capitalists and workers, or Weber and his emphasis on position in the market and opportunities for accumulating wealth from capital or from different occupations, the distinction between status and class is clear. Classes emerge not from the subjective values of community members but from impersonal market dynamics and represent an individual's achieved or inherited economic position. Given participation in the *full range* of economic activities in society, we should expect a group to develop a complete class system. Falling short of full participation, a group may fail to develop some classes.

This was the experience of blacks from the beginning. Restricted in their economic activities, few managed to accumulate substantial wealth, and none entered the ranks of the capitalist upper class. The majority of blacks remained impoverished members of the rural proletariat or the urban unskilled working class. The few who rose above this level were only moderately successful by white standards of their day. Though men such as Spaulding could be found in most major cities with a sizable black population, Kenneth Kusmer's comment about Cleveland around 1915 was true of other cities as well:

> There were no black equivalents to the Swaseys, Mathers, and others who made sections of Euclid Avenue into an exclusive "millionaire's row" at the turn of the century.[13]

Of black business efforts in Chicago, St. Clair Drake and Horace Cayton wrote in 1961 that "despite the multiplication of small capitalists and the greater affluence of some large ones, Negroes have not broken into the industrial and commercial 'big time.'"[14] Long before this, in 1939, Frazier had recognized the futility of black efforts to forge a black capitalist class of entrepreneurs because of the overwhelming obstacles posed by discrimination. He ridiculed the National Negro Business League for "a naive profession of faith in individual thrift and individual enterprise in a world that was rapidly entering a period of corporate wealth."[15]

Given the overwhelming economic homogeneity of blacks, classes were slow in developing during the period from emancipation to the First World War. In the absence of class distinctions similar to those among whites, *status* distinctions predominated. Membership in the emerging black elite depended less on economic means or occupation than on such characteristics as family background, particularly white ancestry, skin color, and manners and morals patterned after middle- and upper-class whites. Without conspicuous economic achievements by a large number of blacks, the early black elite was a very disparate group that included professionals, railroad porters, skilled workers, barbers, headwaiters in white restaurants, and even some servants of wealthy white families. In a 1902 study, Du Bois found the upper status group of blacks in Athens, Georgia, composed of "five teachers, two physicians, three in the United States mail service, three barbers, two tailors, one bookkeeper, two carpenters, two shoemakers, two waiters, one editor, one real estate agent, two ministers, three blacksmiths, one cook, one restaurant keeper, one farmer and one plumber."[16]

The distinction between class and status is not intended to imply, however, that there were no economic differences separating the old black elite from the black masses. The black elite was composed of individuals who as a group had risen above the masses economically as well as socially. Though shoemakers, waiters, cooks, and barbers were not objectively upper-class or even middle-class occupations in the larger society, within the black community of the time they represented steady employment with higher wages than those earned by most other blacks. So rare were such positions among blacks that their very presence set them apart. That they were occupations serving wealthy whites added to their prestige among blacks.

Since the criteria for membership in a status group are a matter of a community's subjective ranking of *available* characteristics as high or low, in time the criteria for membership in the black elite shifted. By the 1920s, most members of the elite—at least in large cities such as Detroit, Chicago, and Cleveland—were professionals or successful (in the eyes of blacks) businessmen. No longer were nonprofessionals such as headwaiters in expensive downtown white restaurants or barbers with wealthy white clienteles considered elite. By this time, however, the old elite had been supplanted in most cities by a new elite dependent on black community patronage rather than on whites for their success.

## THE OLD MULATTO ELITE TAKES ROOT AND EXPANDS: EMANCIPATION TO 1915

The old mulatto elite, with its roots in white society, evolved in part through a paternalistic relationship with upper-class whites that developed in the decades following emancipation. In the South, especially in small towns, white ancestry, a history of freedom before the Civil War, leadership roles in the black church and the local black school, property ownership, and conventional moral behavior were important characteristics affording access to the small circle of the local elite. Such was the emphasis on light complexion that black communities were known to have refused county-appointed teachers who were not mulattoes.[17] The education of the old mulatto elite's children was sometimes promoted through the interest of white relatives or of northern white missionaries who established schools for blacks following emancipation. This white intervention occasionally even led beyond literacy, to an education in a northern Ivy League college and a career as a teacher in the local colored school.

In the larger cities of the South as well as those of northern and border states, craftsmen, caterers, barbers, tailors, and other small businessmen serving the needs of a wealthy white upper class figured prominently in the local black elite. For many, this was simply a continuation of roles assumed by free blacks before the Civil War; for others, these occupations offered the only opportunity to rise above the common condition of the poor black masses. Writing of Detroit in the early post-Civil War years, David Katzman calls barbering the "single most important black business" of that period.[18] This assessment is supported by statistics revealing that although a minority group in the population, in 1870, 43 percent of the barbers in Cleveland, 55 percent in Detroit, and a sizable number in other northern cities were black. Those barbers who managed to become owners of their shops often gained entrance thereby into the black elite.

Caterers and skilled workers were also important elements of the black elite. In some cities, caterers were numerous enough to form organizations or clubs and held elaborate social affairs during the year. Skilled craftsmen were especially important in southern cities, where they often monopolized the trades until forced out by white competition and craft unions during the last decades of the nineteenth century. Because of early competition by white immigrant workers in the North, blacks never gained the same foothold in the crafts that was characteristic in the South, though there were exceptions in cities such as Cleveland, where 32 percent of black males worked as craftsmen in 1870.[19]

Ironically, throughout the late nineteenth century, black professionals were an insignificant element within the black elite. This was due in part to economic and racial barriers to the entry of free blacks into most professional occupations before emancipation and in part to southern mores, which soon defined all but a few professions, such as minister and schoolteacher, as inappropriate for blacks. There was opposition to black lawyers, especially, because of their potential adversarial role vis-á-vis whites. But even doctors and dentists came late to the South, especially in the smaller cities.

James Weldon Johnson wrote of "a strange being [who] came to Jacksonville, [in the 1880s] the first colored doctor."[20] Even in northern cities such as Detroit, black lawyers had a difficult time and were often "professionals without practices,"[21] although in Cleveland, where nineteenth-century race relations were especially mild, many black doctors and lawyers had mixed practices. As Du Bois pointed out in his study of Philadelphia, the failure of black lawyers to prosper was also in part a result of the inability of poor black communities to provide them with opportunities to work and the refusal of whites to employ them.

This discussion of the various occupational elements within the black elite should not be construed to mean that membership in the elite was correlated with occupation. The very occupational diversity of black elites stands in sharp contrast to the greater occupational homogeneity of classes and underscores the fact that other characteristics unified the group. Commenting on black elite "society" in Jacksonville, Florida, in the 1880s, Johnson wrote:

> In the Oceola Club [an elite men's club] a man's occupation had little or nothing to do with his eligibility. Among the members were lawyers, doctors, teachers, bricklayers, carpenters, barbers, waiters, Pullman porters. . . . On one point, this black "society" was precisely like Southern white "society"—anyone belonging to an "old family," regardless of his pecuniary condition or, in fact, his reputation, was eligible.[22]

Such occupational diversity was equally true of northern cities such as Cleveland, where at the turn of the century the black elite included "merchants and small entrepreneurs, skilled craftsmen, barbers who owned their own shops, headwaiters in exclusive establishments, and a few doctors, lawyers, and other professionals."[23]

What especially bound this group together in the face of such diversity was its unique relationship with whites and its life style. The service nature of most of their occupations placed the black elite in daily close contact with wealthy whites, which, even more than the monetary rewards, gave these occupations a high status in the black community.

In the South, early elite contact with whites came in the academies established by northern white missionaries to educate blacks following emancipation. There they received not only a basic education but training in the culture and values of white New England society, training they attempted to follow in later life. Further contact with whites came through domestic work in the homes of wealthy white families and through entrepreneurial services such as barbering and the various crafts. Whenever possible, black elite families sought to live in white neighborhoods, if only on a single block of a street occupied by whites. As the system of segregation tightened in the South the black elite found that intimate contact with whites was disappearing, but they continued to hold fast to the values they had learned from whites through earlier contacts. In time, this imitation became highly formalized and artificial. Writing of this period, Frazier comments:

> because of their isolation, their cultural heritage became ingrown and highly formalized. Therefore, even the most superficial aspects of their culture were often supported by the deepest sentiment. In their social life, social ritual and social graces were often observed with a moral earnestness. And, when one views their creative efforts, their performances appear naive and pitiable. One needs only to read the poetry which this group produced to realize how far their sorry imitations encouched in stilted language and burdened with classical references fell below accepted literary standards.[24]

In the North, black elite contact with whites continued longer than in the South and was considerably more varied. In general, they had good rapport with upper-class and upper-middle-class whites and either had a white clientele or associated with whites through their work. They frequently lived in predominantly white neighborhoods and were likely to have attended the same schools and the same churches. Having adopted the values of white society and culture as their own, the black elite not only strove to emulate the whites with whom they frequently came in contact but also felt the need to separate themselves from the black masses and even the new black elite that began to emerge at the turn of the century. When they no longer attended white churches, they founded high-status congregations, such as St. Matthews Episcopal in Detroit, from which other blacks were excluded. At the turn of the century, the leaders of St. Matthews went so far as to institute pew rentals to discourage other blacks from applying for membership.[25] These churches were distinguished from those of poor blacks by their more sedate and decorous ceremonies. No shouting, emotionalism, or "Amens" graced these walls or encouraged the minister to new heights of eloquence.

Social life centered around exclusive clubs such as the Social Circle in Cleveland or the Sumner Club in Detroit, which was modeled after the predominantly white Michigan Club. There were also various literary societies. The main objective of all these clubs was social, and members regularly entertained in lavish style with parties, dinners, dances, and teas and in general tried to pattern their lives after upper-middle-class whites. A great deal of emphasis was placed on white values and the imitation of affluent whites, an attitude that inclined the black elite to avoid contact with the rank-and-file of black society and to withdraw within the narrow circle of friends and relatives.

In Philadelphia, Washington, D.C., Boston, Chicago, Detroit, Indianapolis, and other cities of the North, this pattern was repeated with slight variations. In Cleveland, some of the more prosperous members of the black elite owned automobiles and went on touring parties to nearby cities with their friends. Most took vacations frequently, sometimes to exclusive black resort areas in the United States and occasionally even to Europe. Children received a great deal of attention and the best education affordable at a southern black college, at Oberlin, or in some cases even at an Ivy League school. For the most part, these were still mulattoes who placed a great deal of emphasis on light complexion and carefully avoided intermarriage with darker blacks. One member of an old mulatto family was discouraged by her mother from any thought of marrying the great black poet, Paul Lawrence Dunbar, because she said a person that black could not become a member of their family—no matter how great a poet he was.[26]

The black elite's disdain for, and embarrassment at, the life style of darker blacks often led to an attitude of blaming the victim. This was especially true when racism increased as northern black communities were swelled by the influx of southern migrants. Many in the elite attributed this rise in racism to failure of other blacks to adopt white standards as they had done. What was needed, one reader of the Cleveland *Advocate* wrote in 1917, was for young blacks to "devote more of their time to literary societies, musical clubs, debating societies, and sewing circles, as was true twenty-five years ago [1892], and less to pool playing, dancing, and playing and other virtue-robbing pleasures" and to "stop their mad rush for pleasure and give more attention to the serious side of life; if they will prepare themselves, perhaps the pendulum for us in the North will swing back, and the privileges we once enjoyed . . . will be restored."[27]

Over time, membership in the old elite changed somewhat as some occupations lost elite status because more and more blacks managed to enter the professions or become successful businessmen. Thus, old family retainers and domestic servants in the wealthier white families ceased to have elite status in the border states by the turn of the century. And in Cleveland as well as in other northern cities, the skilled crafts were no longer considered elite occupations by 1920. Other black elite occupations such as barbershop ownership and head-waiter in an exclusive white establishment were also on the wane because of the competition of immigrant whites and other foreigners for these jobs, which made them less and less accessible to blacks. In Detroit, the percentage of black barbers had declined from 55 per-cent in 1870 to 7.3 percent by 1910. The same pattern could be observed in New York, Cleveland, Chicago, and other northern cities as blacks lost out in competi-tion with white immigrants during a period of mounting racism. While the old elite occupations serving a white clientele were declining in number and prestige, a new group of black entrepreneurs with occupations serving the growing black communities in the North was emerg-ing. These men and women formed the core of a rising *new* black elite that would eventually form a bridge from status groups to classes within the black community.

## THE NEW BLACK ELITE: BRIDGE BETWEEN STATUS AND CLASS

Since the old black elite was so closely connected to white society through service occupations and other contacts, it was precisely the loosening of these pater-nalistic bonds that led to its demise. Deprived of the mainstay of their existence, the old black elite had nowhere to go but toward integration into the black community, a move they strongly resisted. Some of those who finally accepted the inevitable found that other blacks had preceded them in forging a base within the black community and had established the elements of a new elite unconcerned about acceptance by whites or the old elite.

A number of simultaneous developments during the last decades of the nineteenth century and up to about 1915 contributed to a weakening of the old elite's ties with white society. In the first place, the relationship had been a paternalistic one, largely based on service to a wealthy white clientele. In some cities of the North, there were also political benefits to be reaped through association with a Republican-controlled political system still committed to the ideals of Reconstruction. Members of the black elite were recognized in such cities as the official representatives of black society and were often able to find jobs for their sons in public service. But as the Republican party lost interest in reconstruction and sought a rapprochement with southern whites, these political channels into white society began to dry up, and old leaders began losing their legitimacy and access to patronage jobs.

As mentioned above, this was also a period of increased racism and competition from white immigrants for many of the occupations that had contributed to the growth of the old black elite in earlier days. These and other elite occupations serving a white clientéle were rapidly declining among blacks by the turn of the century. By 1918, only two important restaurants in Cleveland employed black waiters, and the proportion of black males in skilled trades had declined to 11.1 percent in 1910 from a high of 32 percent in 1870. These trends were universal throughout the cities of the North.

The most important factor in the decline of the old elite's relationship to white society, on which it depended for its existence, was the rise of a new white upper class at the end of the nineteenth century and beginning of the twentieth century. These nouveau riches themselves suffered from a certain amount of status anxiety as they challenged the securer and more genteel old white elite. In their anxiety, they began distancing themselves from the rest of society and from the old black elite by moving to residentially exclusive areas of the city or suburbs and by establishing clubs, private schools, and other institutions that further shielded them from contact with others.

## RISE OF THE NEW BLACK ELITE

While increased racism and the occupational competition of white immigrants led to a decline in old elite jobs, these forces also set the stage for the appearance of new occupations serving the black community exclusively. As migrants from the South gradually increased the size of black urban communities, blacks experienced increased difficulty in finding white realtors who would sell or rent property to them. White insurance agents began refusing to sell policies to blacks, and banks frequently turned down their loan applications. Even white funeral parlors showed reluctance to bury their dead. Since these were some of the most basic needs of a growing black community, ambitious black entrepreneurs, seeing an opportunity to fill a void, began entering these fields. Also, in every major city, black newspapers sprang up to meet the needs of growing black communities for black-oriented news and for coverage of social events that never made the white dailies. Some of these ghetto-based entrepreneurs became very successful.

Many black professionals also began profiting from the refusal of whites to accept black clients. In general, this aided the practices of black doctors and dentists more than those of black lawyers, although the growth of black businesses provided black lawyers with increased opportunities also. Thus, beginning around the turn of the century, an emerging new elite began to replace the old elite within the black community. What especially distinguished this new elite of realtors, insurance agents, undertakers, bankers, newspaper editors, politicians, and professionals was their orientation to, and dependency on, black community patronage. As a group, they showed little interest in cultivating close ties with whites, as the old elite had done; nor did they exhibit the old elite's snobbishness toward the black masses. While they, too, founded social clubs for their own entertainment, many functioned as benevolent organizations to help poor blacks.

By 1915, this new black elite had replaced the old elite everywhere; it was now at the top of the social pyramid within the black community. At the same time, because they did not exhibit the occupational diversity of the old elite—or its exclusivity—but consisted primarily of businessmen and professionals, they formed the core of an emerging black middle class, serving as a bridge between a black community dominated by status groups to one characterized by classes. That is, position at the top of the black community could now be secured through economic achievement rather than through family background, skin color, or white approval.

## What Happened to the Old Elite?

This new orientation was so much at variance with the values of the old elite that it should not be surprising to learn its members witnessed these changes with both alarm and disdain for these newcomers. For a long time, they kept themselves apart in their exclusive clubs, friendship cliques, and churches. Even when their num-

bers began to decline through the disappearance of
service-oriented jobs and such natural causes as small
family size, childlessness, unmarried children, and out-
migration, some still refused to associate with members
of the new elite. But many, bowing to the inevitable,
gradually intermarried with the more successful dark-
skinned middle-class black males whose position in the
community came from a college education and a white-
collar job rather than from membership in an old family.
At the same time, status-conscious dark-skinned middle-class males, however, often sought to enhance their
standing in the community through marriage to a mulatto woman from an old family. Frazier quotes a black
college professor with origins in the unskilled working
class as saying of his blond wife, "You see my wife. I
married her so that there would be no question about
the status of my family. She has the right skin color and,
more than that, comes from an old family."[28] Thus, a
kind of merger of convenience took place by which old
elite families found economically successful husbands
for their daughters within the ranks of the rising middle
class and dark black males, new to the middle class,
found a way to shore up their status in the community.
The continued emphasis on skin color, Frazier argues,
was largely the result of the presence of old elite mulatto
families within the growing middle class; those with
working class and farm origins were more concerned
with economic success. Out of this merger of convenience there began to develop during the early decades
of the twentieth century what Frazier called a "brown
middle class."[29] In fact, as a class, the emerging black
middle class (which I shall refer to as the *old middle class*)
was very diverse in terms of family background and
skin color. It drew from various segments of the black
population as the sons and daughters of farmers,
domestics, laborers, factory workers, teachers, doctors,
undertakers, and realtors moved into the middle class

through the achievement of a white-collar occupation following their years in college. They were dark, brown skinned, and mulatto. The mixtures created great diversity in the pigmentation of children—even within the same family—for the coming generations, although for a long time there remained a fixation on light skin complexion.

## OCCUPATIONAL RESTRICTIONS WITHIN THE OLD MIDDLE CLASS

At this point, on the eve of the First World War, the range of occupations within the emerging black middle class was considerably restricted and was to remain so for a long time to come. Though the new entrepreneurial occupations serving the black community, such as real estate agent, banker, insurance salesman, undertaker, and newspaper editor, were important and prestigious, they did not exist in large numbers. Far more numerous than those in all of the above occupations combined were those finding jobs as elementary and secondary schoolteachers in the new schools being established for blacks in many northern cities or in schools already existing in the South. Ministers formed the second largest (or even the largest in some cities) professional category.

In an analysis of the occupational distribution of black workers in fifteen cities of the South, the North, and border states in 1920, Frazier found that clergymen predominated among black professionals in the South but were less numerous in other regions. In Atlanta and Birmingham, over half of all professionals were ministers, while in other southern cities their numbers ranged from more than one in three to one out of every two professionals. At the other extreme, only one in ten black professionals in Boston and New York were clergymen.[30] As Allan Spear points out, to make matters worse, black clergymen during this period ranked among the least educated of all black professionals.[31]

As was to be the case in the decades to come, blacks experienced extreme difficulty in penetrating other middle-class occupations in both the North and South. This had been true in the final decades of the nineteenth century when the old black elite dominated the black community without challenge and remained true as it lost its grip and was replaced by a new elite and an emerging black middle class during the first decade and a half of the twentieth century. Everywhere blacks found the newer engineering fields closed to them, black journalists could find few openings outside the black weeklies, and it was practically impossible for blacks to find clerical jobs in white establishments, in spite of the rapid increase in such work during this period. The majority of female clerical jobs went to native-born white women. In Detroit in 1910, there were no blacks among the 1,186 telephone operators, one black among the 2,081 saleswomen in stores, and only ten blacks among the 7,106 office clerical workers. Katzman suggests that even these few clerical workers probably worked in black businesses.[32] Of the nearly 15,000 male clerical workers during that same year in Detroit, only forty-six were black. The experiences of blacks seeking clerical jobs were the same in the other cities of the North. Black males found it equally difficult to be hired as firemen, policemen, or streetcar conductors—a situation that led D. A. Straker, a black lawyer in Detroit, to lament in 1910:

> He may be a janitor, but cannot be a clerk; he may be a porter on a steam-car, but not a conductor; he may sweep the lawyer's office, but cannot become his law-partner, his typewriter, or his stenographer; he may buy of the merchant, but cannot become his clerk; he may carry the hod, but cannot contract for the building.[33]

Only in public service jobs in the North, particularly as postal clerks or carriers, were blacks able to secure clerical work outside of black businesses.

When we examine national statistics for the distribution of black workers in 1910, we discover that less than one percent were in clerical and sales positions, about the same number were proprietors and managers (primarily small businessmen), and only about 1.5 percent held professional jobs (fig. 2). It is important to note that clerical and sales workers constituted the single largest category within the white middle class, while among blacks, professionals were in the majority at this time. This was entirely the result of existing patterns of occupational discrimination. As a result of these restrictions, the early development of the old black middle class was distorted and came to differ significantly from patterns existing among whites.


## THE OLD BLACK MIDDLE CLASS GROWS: 1915–1960

To understand fully the uniqueness of the old black middle class, each of the major occupational groups within the class will be examined separately, beginning with black entrepreneurs.

### THE RISE AND FALL OF HOPE
### FOR A BLACK CAPITALIST CLASS

At the outset, we should carefully distinguish a capitalist upper class in the Marxian (and Weberian) sense, as discussed in the introduction, from a stratum of small businessmen (the petite bourgeoisie). Both aspirations have existed among blacks, with the former completely frustrated and the latter never reaching the level of success found among white ethnics. When the Fourth Atlanta University Conference on "The Negro in

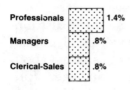

Fig. 2. Distribution of middle-class black and white workers by strata in 1910 as percentage of total black and white labor forces.

Business" met in 1898 with 1,906 black businessmen attending, John Hope, a future president of Atlanta University, expressed the sentiment that black economic development depended on the emergence of a black capitalist class whose businesses would provide jobs for black workers. Two years later, Booker T. Washington founded the National Negro Business League to promote that goal. Although it grew rapidly and could count six hundred local leagues by 1915, Frazier was later to ridicule them for "a naive profession of faith in individual thrift and individual enterprise in a world that was rapidly entering a period of corporate wealth."[34] However, Frazier had earlier held this same hope for the development of a black capitalist class. In an article written for Alain Locke's *The New Negro* in 1925, he showed great enthusiasm for black entrepreneurial developments in Durham. Calling Durham the "capital of the black middle class," Frazier wrote, "No longer can men say that the Negro is lazy and shiftless and a consumer. He has gone to work. He is a producer. He is respectable. He has a middle class." And of these entrepreneurs there could be told "stories paralleling the most amazing accounts of the building of American fortunes."[35]

Why do we find Frazier changing his assessment of the potential for a black capitalist class so drastically just fourteen years later? The answer lies in his gradual understanding of the types of businesses blacks had been able to develop. Though the number of black-owned businesses seemed to grow impressively from about 1,900 in 1898 to 70,000 in 1930, the majority were small establishments in the area of personal service: barbershops, beauty parlors, cleaners, tailors, restaurants, and grocery stores. Of Chicago's 2,600 black businesses in 1938, Drake and Cayton found that the five most numerous were beauty parlors, grocery stores, barbershops, tailors, cleaners and pressers, and restaurants. The next five most numerous were coal and wood dealers, taverns, undertakers, shoe repairing, and dressmakers.[36] A national survey of black-owned businesses about ten years later (1946) had similar findings. It not only showed that the majority were service oriented (48%) but that 85 percent were owned by one person, and 81 percent were located in black neighborhoods.[37]

Since the turn of the century, the growth of black urban populations had been the catalyst for black business development by creating a market. The nature of these businesses, however, was largely dictated by patterns of discrimination faced by the black population. Since discrimination was keenest in the areas of personal services, black entrepreneurs found their greatest opportunities in filling this need. This produced the characterization of black businesses as "defensive enterprises."[38] No black wholesale businesses were found in the twelve cities covered by the 1946 survey. And of the only nineteen businesses engaged in manufacturing, thirteen made either caskets or cosmetics. Nor did black entrepreneurs prove much more successful in the area of banking, though they were able to develop a number of long-lived insurance companies.

When compared with white businesses, even the successes pale considerably. It was estimated by Joseph Pierce in 1947 that one large white insurance company had policies on black customers amounting to more than twice the amount of the insurance held by all forty-four black insurance companies combined. In Chicago, whites not only owned the largest business establishments in black neighborhoods in 1938 but their total numbers exceeded the 2,600 black businesses by 200 and they received more than 90 percent of all money spent by blacks in the ghetto. Apart from the larger size of white businesses, a reason for their greater monetary success was that more were concentrated in areas of basic need, such as grocery stores, meat markets, bakeries, coal and ice companies, restaurants, and clothing, department, and furniture stores. Black retailers often complained about the lack of patronage by blacks while black consumers pointed to their higher prices, failure to extend credit, and more restricted selection of goods. Newspaper editors, ministers, and community leaders all urged the community to "buy black," arguing that in so doing, they would enable black businessmen to turn a profit as well as provide jobs for blacks. This doctrine of the "double-duty dollar," which according to Drake and Cayton was widespread at the time, expressed an unrealistic belief in the ability of black businesses to provide jobs.

In Cleveland, a 1929 survey had found that most of the 215 existing black businesses were owned by single individuals and employed only 161 full-time and 34 part-time employees.[39] Much the same patterns were observed in Harlem and other cities in both the North and South. Most black businesses were small ventures unable to secure adequate capital from white banks and unable to compete with large white firms and chain stores offering lower prices, a wider selection of goods, and using expensive advertising campaigns. Almost the only notable success came in areas where black entrepreneurs held a virtual monopoly, such as the undertaking business, the black cosmetic industry, and real estate. In the cosmetic industry, Madame C. J. Walker made a small fortune on beauty products that promised black women "the thrill of lighter, fairer, brighter, younger-looking skin."[40] But in spite of some success, in the last analysis, black entrepreneurs were not able to penetrate the ranks of corporate America or even become a major force among the petite bourgeoisie stratum of the middle class. By 1960, this stratum, which included black managers and officials, had grown from less than 1 percent of the black labor force to only 1.4 percent, compared to 9.1 percent among whites (fig. 3). Frazier argued that the major reason for this failure was discrimination. Writing of black businessmen in Durham, he commented, "Had it not been for the bar of color some of them would have been counted among the most conspicuous of the new industrial and commercial classes in the South."[41]

BLACK PROFESSIONALS: SERVICE TO THE REJECTED

As in the case of black businessmen, the rapid rise of black urban communities together with the reluctance, or even refusal, of white professionals to serve blacks provided the opportunity for growth in the number of black professionals. This stratum is unique within the middle class in that preparation for professional occupations requires the expenditure of considerable time and

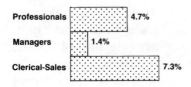

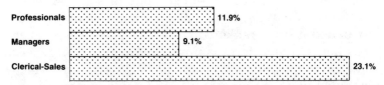

Fig. 3. Distribution of middle-class black and white workers by strata in 1960 as percentage of total black and white labor forces.

money to acquire an advanced professional or graduate degree or at least four years to acquire an undergraduate degree. For blacks, there has always been the additional problem of finding opportunities to secure employment once a degree is acquired. The latter problem, especially, resulted in the concentration of blacks in relatively few occupations, primarily the ministry, teaching, medicine, dentistry, social work, and law.

## PROFESSIONAL AND GRADUATE EDUCATION

Carter G. Woodson's study of black professionals in 1934 revealed that while blacks rushed to enter professional fields following emancipation, the opportunities for realizing such ambitions remained very limited until far into the twentieth century.[42] Though blacks had long attended professional and graduate schools in a number of universities in the North and Midwest, the cost of such an education was out of the reach of all but northern old elite black families and a few elite families in the South. While Oberlin, the University of Michigan, and Harvard welcomed blacks, few managed to enter.

In the South, where the majority of blacks lived, graduate training was not available to blacks until Howard University began a formal program in 1921.[43] This initiative was followed in 1927 by Fisk and Hampton Institute, in 1929 and 1933 by Atlanta and Xavier, and in 1937 and 1938 by Virginia State and Prairie View. Most of the 448 regular graduate students enrolled in these schools in 1938 were preparing for a career in education, the area offering the greatest opportunities for trained professional employment in the South. During the 1938–39 academic year, another 20 percent studied English and slightly less than 20 percent, history. Of the 686 master's degrees awarded between 1919 and 1938 by all of these schools except Prairie View, half were awarded by Howard University.

Professional education developed even slower than graduate education in the black universities. By 1945, Howard alone had all the traditional professional schools: medicine, dentistry, pharmacy, law, social work, and theology, although others developed professional programs in some areas and even became distinguished. These included the school of pharmacy at Xavier University in New Orleans, social work at Atlanta, and medicine at Meharry Medical College in Nashville. All, whether public or private, had great difficulty finding enough financial support to meet the needs of first-rate graduate and professional training. Only Howard—because of the historical accident of having received federal funds since its founding—was able to succeed in developing something like adequate training. Other black colleges received only minor contributions. For example, during the 1935–36 academic year, black colleges received only slightly more than $260,000 compared to almost $3,000,000 received by white colleges. Because of the low level of funding, black higher education—the source of the professional stratum—lagged far behind that of whites. By 1960, only 3 percent of all blacks 25 years old and over had completed four or more years of college, compared to 8 percent of whites in the same age group. Of these 9,054 black graduates, 57 percent lived in the South.

## PROFESSIONALS ON THE FRINGES

Those blacks who managed to overcome the many obstacles to a professional education emerged into a world in which they occupied a very ambiguous position. Though bona fide, trained professionals, their activities were severely circumscribed by the racial norms of a still very segregated society. In practice, this meant that having taken the Hippocratic oath and trained to heal bodies in need of their skills, black doctors could only minister to bodies with black skins. So, too, black dentists were restricted to serving black patients. And while the growth of urban black communities in the North and South after 1915 provided black doctors and lawyers with increased opportunities for employment, black lawyers made the least progress. This was a result, in part, of the problem of finding adequate clients among the poor black masses on whom they depended for livelihood; in part, of the prejudices of educated blacks against black professionals; and, in part, of racial norms in the South which tended to restrict blacks in the professions to "teaching, preaching, and the practice of medicine." Of the plight of the black lawyer in the South, Woodson wrote:

A Negro lawyer is not in good standing in the majority
of the states of the South except in a few large cities
where the public is more liberal-minded. In certain parts
he would not be permitted to appear in the court under
any circumstances to undertake to try a case. His life
would be in danger if he tried to override public opinion
which proscribes the Negro in this sphere.[44]

The position of the black lawyer during this period
becomes even clearer when his income is compared
with that of other professionals. In 1928, the average
income of black lawyers was only $1,500, compared to
$2,000 for black dentists and $2,500 for black doctors.
The incomes of black doctors, although the highest
among black professionals, were still far below the
$8,784 average for white doctors. It is not surprising,
then, to learn that black lawyers frequently had to hold
a second job to make ends meet.

Most numerous among black professionals were
teachers and ministers. The former found job opportunities in the segregated schools of the South and the
North and received their incomes from the state. Ministers also did not have to depend on the economic resources of individual black clients and were responding
to the needs of a deeply religious people. While opportunities for employment were more numerous in these
professions than all others combined, they, too, were
underpaid and, like lawyers, frequently had to hold a
second job to earn a decent living. The salaries of black
teachers in southern and border states, where the majority lived, never reached more than two-thirds that of
whites in North Carolina and were as low as 37 and 32
percent of the salaries of white teachers in South
Carolina and Georgia in the 1930s.

Black ministers, as I pointed out above, were among
the least educated of all professionals. Many had either

minimal or no formal theological training and were, in fact, self-appointed preachers who, having "received the call," attracted a following and opened a church. In the emerging ghettos of the North, religious expression took the form of storefront churches in which black migrants from the South sought the communal warmth they had left behind. Though their religious fervor often prompted congregations to give generously for the support of their minister, the small size and poverty of many of them frequently made these contributions little more than the proverbial widow's mite. As a result, black ministers, the majority of whom served poor blacks, were themselves often as poor as the members of their flock. Only in the few churches serving middle-class blacks were ministers well educated and financially well-off.

The severe restrictions faced by black professionals—lack of opportunities for acquiring a professional education, an impoverished black community, prejudices among educated blacks, racial and exclusionary norms—resulted in a slow and uneven growth in the number and types of black professionals between 1915 and 1960. Nationally, only 1.5 percent of all black workers were professionals in 1920, compared to more than 5 percent of all whites. A decade later, while the proportion of black professionals had increased to 2.1 percent, whites increased their numbers even faster, so the gap between blacks and whites in the professions actually widened. Of the 135,964 black professionals and semiprofessionals in 1930, Woodson found that almost one-half were teachers. The next most numerous categories were clergymen (18%) and musicians and music teachers (7.8%). Together, these three professions accounted for about two-thirds of all black professionals. Physicians, lawyers, judges, and dentists together amounted to only 5 percent of all professionals.[45]

Both the number and types of black professionals

differed significantly between the North and South as the North proved to be a much more fertile ground for the development of a black middle class. Summarizing his findings about the distributions of black professionals in the 1930s, Woodson wrote:

> The large majority of the Negroes in the professions are found in the South, but not in proportion to the population. One will sometimes find more professional Negroes in one Northern city than in a whole state in the South. This peculiar distribution is often due to racial antagonism and oppression.[46]

The majority of black teachers, preachers, physicians, and nurses were located in the South during the 1930s and the majority of lawyers, dentists, musicians, and music teachers were located in the North. Woodson found that Illinois, with a black population of only 328,972, had more black doctors than Alabama, Arkansas, and South Carolina, which had a combined black population of 2,216,978. Similarly, Pennsylvania, with only 431,257 blacks, had more dentists than Arkansas, Georgia, Mississippi, and South Carolina, with 3,352,987 blacks. Finally, 40 percent of all black doctors served only 19 percent of the total black population residing in New Jersey, New York, Pennsylvania, Ohio, Michigan, Illinois, Missouri, and the District of Columbia in 1933. The more fertile conditions for the development of a black middle class in the North can also be seen from the higher proportions of black professionals in cities of northern and border states compared with those in the deep South. Comparing eleven cities with black populations of 100,000 or more, Frazier found that in 1940 the southern cities of Birmingham and Memphis had proportions as low as 2 percent and 2.2 percent, respectively, while in New York, black professional representation reached a high of 3.5 percent, followed by 3.3 percent in Chicago and St. Louis.[47]

## CLERICAL AND SALES WORKERS

While sociologists today debate whether clerical workers should continue to be included within the middle class or whether their working condition has deteriorated to such an extent that they are now members of the working class, there is no doubt that from the 1920s through the 1950s, clerical and sales jobs offered significant opportunities for upward mobility and prestige. Not only were these "clean" jobs requiring mental rather than physical work and often commanding higher salaries but during periods when most workers were still engaged in either agricultural or manual labor, clerical and sales positions represented the achievement of relatively few within the American labor force. Thus, it could be expected that competition for these jobs would be keen and that it would be an area of the economy where discrimination would be high both in the North and the South. Unlike professionals and those in business, clerical and sales personnel were salaried workers and thus completely dependent on the willingness of employers to hire them.

In the South, where most black workers could still be found, cultural norms dictated that no black individual could occupy a clerical or sales position in white establishments, since these occupations were associated with a social status to which black workers could not aspire. The idea of blacks engaged in clean work in the front offices of establishments serving a white public was completely repugnant to white sentiments and effectively prevented blacks from occupying such positions. Neither could blacks find much clerical and sales work in black businesses, since, because of their small size, they had relatively little need for clerical help. The only exceptions were Atlanta and New Orleans, where the presence of a number of black colleges created a greater need for clerical work in black establishments than elsewhere in the South. During the 1920s, a period when the number of these jobs was increasing rapidly in cities such as Chicago, Drake and Cayton reported that while "forty per cent of the new white women workers went into 'clean work,' . . . only five per cent of the Negro women secured such jobs."[48] Those blacks who did manage to find such work were able to do so only in the black ghetto, in the federal government, especially the postal service, or, to a more limited extent, in local governments. In fact, with its standardized entrance exams, the postal service provided blacks in the North with their first major opportunity for lower-level white-collar work. It is an area of government in which blacks have continued to remain concentrated to this day.

In private businesses, the color line remained firm except in periods of acute labor shortage such as the First World War. Even then, stores that hired black clerks did so only on a temporary basis, firing them at the end of the war. In general, native whites were the most successful in the competition for the new clerical jobs, but even foreign-born whites fared better than blacks. In Cleveland in 1930, 46 percent of female native whites in the labor force and 20 percent of foreign-born whites had secured clerical jobs, compared to less than 3 percent of black females. Similar disparities existed among males in clerical work.

In his study of eleven cities with a black population of 100,000 or more, plus Louisville, Kentucky, Frazier found that the proportion of blacks in clerical work was still very low in 1940. This was especially true of the four southern cities (Atlanta, Birmingham, Memphis, and New Orleans), where he found only 2.5 to 5 percent holding clerical jobs. Larger numbers of blacks managed to secure clerical work in the four cities of the border states (Baltimore, St. Louis, Louisville, and Washington, D.C.), particularly in Washington, D.C., where opportunities for work in the federal government raised the proportion to almost 10 percent—a proportion approached or exceeded only in northern cities such as New York, Chicago, Philadelphia, and Detroit.

The difficulty blacks experienced in being hired for clerical work had a significant impact on their class structure and especially on the development of a middle class. In the most comprehensive study of occupational mobility in the United States ever attempted, Blau and Duncan found in 1962 that the lower-middle-class stratum (clerical and sales) serves as both an entree into the middle class for upwardly mobile individuals and as a buffer for downwardly mobile sons of upper-middle-class families. In other words, sons of fathers in the professions or in business who could not themselves secure similar jobs chose to seek clerical or sales work rather than blue-collar jobs—even when the latter commanded higher entry-level salaries.[49] Among females, who traditionally experienced discrimination in their attempts to enter most professional and business careers, clerical work became the focus of their middle-class aspirations. As a result, among whites, the clerical stratum has always exceeded in size the professional and entrepreneurial strata combined. In contrast, among blacks, this "natural" development in the structure of the middle class has been distorted by their limited access historically to clerical and sales jobs. It was not until the 1940s, when efforts by the Urban League and other black organizations to end the color bar in northern cities at last began to succeed, that the proportion of black clerical and sales workers exceeded that of black professionals for the first time. And it was about 1960 before the gap between the proportion of blacks and whites in the clerical-sales stratum began to narrow. Thus, while white society allowed blacks to enter those middle-class occupations which directly served the needs of the black population, they continued to oppose entry into areas involving service to whites and competition with whites.

## COPING WITH EXCLUSION: LIFE BEHIND
## THE WALLS OF SEGREGATION

How did middle-class blacks cope with the dilemma of their position in American society? Here were individuals who by training, occupation, and, sometimes, economic achievement had attained the symbols of success generally respected in society but were continuously reminded in a variety of ways that because of the color of their skin they were not seen as equal to their peers and were, in fact, frequently treated as inferior. In the South, middle-class blacks—like blacks of all classes—were forced to "stay in their place," a phrase that meant, among other things, riding in the back of the bus, sitting in the balcony of theaters, using "colored only" water fountains and waiting rooms, and denial of access to restaurants, hotels, parks, and other amusement places. The difficulty in finding lodging when traveling across the country led to the publication of *The Negro Motorist Green Book* by Victor Green, a World War I veteran. Begun in 1936 as an annual, the *Green Book* contained information on lodging—tourist homes and small hotels—for the black traveler. The 1946 edition, which I have, marked its reappearance following suspension during the Second World War and covers the entire United States. In addition to lodging, it lists the location of "friendly" service stations, restaurants, barbershops, beauty parlors, taverns, garages, night clubs, and tailors accepting black customers. Most of the accessible lodgings in 1946 were still tourist homes rather than hotels.

Although such a resource was indispensable in the South, it was also useful in the North where middle-class blacks faced the dilemma of the unexpected; at times, they were not at all sure how to behave or how whites would behave toward them. They experienced the conflict of a fixed status in some areas of life and the right to compete in others. Commenting on the middle-class black's plight in Chicago, Drake and Cayton wrote:

> He may be awarded a degree from a university, but he cannot expect to practice medicine in a white hospital, or be pledged to a white fraternity, or attend the senior formal dance—at least under ordinary circumstances.[50]

They give numerous examples of the indignities suffered by blacks on beaches and in bars, hotels, and restaurants. For example, the following occurred in the late 1930s:

> Two colored school teachers and several white friends attended a luncheon at an exclusive coffee shop. The Negro women were allowed to sit down, but the waitress ignored them and served the white women. One of the colored women protested and was told that she could eat in the kitchen.[51]

Faced with these experiences, middle-class blacks had two options: circle the wagons and attempt to develop their own way of life apart from both mainstream white society and the black masses or attempt to gain acceptance, equality, and full participation in the institutional life of the larger society. The first is a defensive strategy stemming from repeated negative experiences and rebuffs from white society; the second is offensive. And while both strategies were used over time, during this period of the emergence of the old black middle class, the emphasis was on the former. Though in many ways understandable, it was this defensive posture that led Frazier to accuse the black middle class of actually opposing integration for fear it would put an end to the advantages and comfortable way of life that many had been able to develop at the top of the social and class pyramids of the black community.

## OF CASTLES AND CLUBS

Denied ready access to the recreational and cultural facilities in the community, middle-class blacks developed a life style largely centered around home and clubs. The home grew in importance not only as a comfortable, secure place that shielded them from the stings of white society but also as the center of their social life. Every attempt was made to become homeowners, and homes were furnished as lavishly as possible, for example, with linen, glassware, china, and silver. While their incomes were far lower than the incomes of their white counterparts, most were fair for their day (often acquired through the combined work efforts of both spouses and sometimes other family members as well), and thus they were able to entertain frequently. Drake and Cayton described in detail the life style of this class in Chicago, but the description is applicable in other cities as well.[52]

Upper-middle-class wives formed small, exclusive social cliques, most often centered around bridge playing, which many engaged in several times a week. Some of these cliques were formalized into exclusive social clubs, which took care to screen prospective members. One member of a bridge club in Chicago, the Monday Night Bridge Club, described their selection process as follows:

The enrollment never exceeds sixteen. New members are admitted only upon unanimous vote. The woman in question is contacted by some one member of the club

who is interested in having her enrolled. Her name is
then presented individually to each member. Then it is
brought before the entire club for a vote. As we wish to
avoid any sort of embarrassment which group discussion of the proposed member might arouse, we approach each member privately to test attitudes.[53]

Upper-middle-class men sometimes participated in
mixed-group clubs but also belonged to all-male clubs.
Unlike the women's clubs, their meetings included discussions as well as entertainment, and they usually
sponsored several large affairs during the year, such as
picnics, suppers, and, especially, dances. The dances
were given prominent coverage in the local black newspaper, with each club attempting to outdo the others in
the lavishness of these events, which also served as the
standard for entertainment in other classes. While most
male clubs were small and also preoccupied with exclu-
siveness, there were some with several hundred members. These large clubs maintained clubhouses where
their members gathered to talk, play poker, read, and
argue race and politics.

Within the lower middle class there was a prolifera-
tion of social clubs growing out of friendship cliques
with such catchy names as the "Amicable Twelve,"
"Peppy Ten," "Jolly Brownettes," "Bronzeville Debs,"
"Les Jolies Douze," "Casanova Boys," and "Las Amigas
Señoras." Most were composed of women, though
there were mixed clubs and a number of all-male clubs.
They competed for the spotlight, had their events published in the black newspaper, and tried to outdo each
other in the grandeur of the annual dance. Thus, a way
of life developed within the black middle class which
was not dependent on access to white restaurants,
clubhouses, or hotel facilities. It was a parallel society
of which whites were largely ignorant and in which
they had little interest. It was also a way of life that

Frazier criticized in the mid-1950s for what he called its shallowness, its preoccupation with "society," and its conspicuous consumption beyond their means. He argued that these men and women, who were in reality middle class by occupation, thought of themselves as upper class or even aristocracy and tried to emulate the consumption patterns of upper-middle-class and upper-class whites.[54] "A teacher or physician is not simply a professional worker," he wrote, "but generally regards himself as a member of an aristocracy which requires certain standards of consumption."[55]

## AND BUTTERFLIES

There is no doubt that much of Frazier's criticism was valid, though black writers continue to debate the degree or extent of its accuracy. Drake and Cayton, in their study of black life in Chicago up to the Second World War, took note of criticism of middle-class social life and values from within the class itself, criticism that accused some of "frivolity," referring to them as the "butterfly group." Such criticism usually came from women and men who participated in activities and organizations aimed at "uplift" and "racial advancement." One woman officer in a club whose members devoted their attention to improving conditions for blacks remarked:

> There is first of all the group which we might term the "butterfly group." What we call the "Society" group in Chicago and most of our large urban centers is made up largely of the "butterfly" type of person—people who play bridge four or five times a week, who belong to social clubs only, and who do not do any constructive work in the community except perhaps once or twice a year.[56]

To be sure, there was considerable preoccupation within the black middle class with maintaining the correct "front" and with "respectability," but there were also the civic-minded, or "Race Women" and "Race Men," as they were called. While in the minority, their numbers were large enough to have an impact. They were the men and women who formed and led such organizations as the NAACP, the Urban League, and other local groups whose primary interest was civic rather than social. They attempted, and often succeeded, in goading the more frivolous to participate in civic activities, especially fund raising. They became the community leaders who were recognized and often looked up to by the black community and those who maintained contacts with sympathetic whites who could be persuaded to help the black cause. These were also the men and women who developed parallel institutions in the black community to serve the needs of black people denied access to white institutions.

## CONTRIBUTIONS OF THE OLD
## BLACK MIDDLE CLASS

During this period, blacks of all classes found themselves denied access to, or service from, most of the institutions that served the everyday needs of the larger community, including education, health care, communication, professional development, and church affiliation. In some cases, this discrimination took on a peculiar twist, as in the case of the medical schools of the University of Chicago and Northwestern University which accepted one or two black doctors on their faculties while denying admission to black medical students. Black doctors, lawyers, dentists, and schoolteachers, regardless of the schools from which they graduated, found themselves excluded from the major professional organizations in the North as well as the South. The essential services of health care and education, when available, were provided on a segregated basis only in the South and frequently in the North. And blacks of all classes found that almost the only news reported about blacks in the white newspapers was of a negative character.

It was during this period that the parallel institutions of the black community were created by the emerging black middle class. Newspapers were founded in most large cities to report news of interest to the black community. Many of these were short-lived; but a surprising number in the largest cities have survived to this day, including, for instance, the Chicago *Defender*, New York City's *Amsterdam News*, and Washington's *Afro-American*. Doctors, lawyers, dentists, schoolteachers, and other professionals started their own local and national professional organizations to promote the development of their respective members. And generations of blacks were educated at all levels owing to the dedication of black teachers in schools that were underfunded and ill-equipped. Many blacks who later made it into the middle class were able to do so only because of those black teachers who had been willing to toil in crowded one- or two-room schoolhouses in the South while their white counterparts worked in large, well-equipped buildings or who experienced varying forms of slights and discrimination in the increasingly segregated school systems of the North. It was largely because of their heroic efforts that the high illiteracy rate among blacks declined steadily from 33 percent in 1910 to 7 percent in 1959. When viewed against the rates among whites during this same period—5 percent in 1910 and 2 percent in 1959—it becomes clear what a significant achievement this was.

But it was especially in the development of a system of higher education, both public and private, throughout the South and parts of the Midwest that the black middle class achieved its greatest success in creating parallel institutions for the growth and development of the black community. I have already discussed the odds they struggled against—inadequate funding, poor equipment, low salaries, and heavy teaching loads—to turn out generations of college-educated blacks who would not otherwise have had an opportunity to move up the American class ladder. The few blacks who attended Ivy League schools in the North were always the exception. Although many private and some public universities in the North accepted blacks, only a few upper-middle-class black families could afford to send their sons and daughters to these expensive schools. Without the system of black colleges and universities, there would not have been an adequate supply of black doctors, dentists, lawyers, social workers, and teachers to serve the needs of the black community. Without this system of higher education, there would have been little opportunity for the sons and daughters of sharecroppers, laborers, Pullman porters, domestics, and factory workers to participate in the phenomenon of upward mobility that characterized white American society. Without this system of higher education, the number of black college students would not have reached the critical mass needed to help spearhead the civil rights movement. To a large degree because of this system, the proportion of blacks with four years or more of college rose from 1 percent in 1940 to 3 percent in 1960, compared to 5 and 8 percent, respectively, for whites.

Unfortunately, the success achieved in developing a black educational system—limited though it was—could not be matched in the economic area. During the first half of the twentieth century, middle-class blacks repeatedly attempted to develop a variety of financial institutions and insurance companies to meet the needs of a growing black community experiencing difficulty in obtaining loans and insurance from white institutions. Except for a few insurance companies, most of these black institutions were short-lived. Efforts to create black business enterprises met with a similar fate in spite of frequent "buy black" campaigns, the exhortations of ministers from the pulpit, and the creation of the "double-duty dollar" ideology. Only in the areas of real estate, funeral parlors, and the manufacturing of cosmetics were blacks able to achieve a measure of success. To be sure, aspiring black entrepreneurs often lacked experience in business, but discrimination by financial institutions, the competition of better-financed white merchants and chain stores, and the futility of appealing to the white market were the major causes of most failures. As a consequence, efforts to develop a black entrepreneurial class were frustrated. In cities like Chicago, New York, and Detroit where the greatest opportunities existed, blacks did not manage to accumulate any real wealth or become members of the board of trade, chamber of commerce, or other influential economic organizations.

This is not to deny the significant, though modest (by white standards), achievements of many black merchants, doctors, lawyers, and other professionals and entrepreneurs. Black doctors and dentists not only were there to meet the health needs of growing black urban communities but a number of black doctors also distinguished themselves in their fields. Many of the basic needs of the black community depended on the existence of black professionals for their total or partial fulfillment.

Middle-class blacks also provided the leadership needed by the black community. In the North, some members of the black middle class were elected to public office from black districts and were able to represent the interests of blacks in a formal capacity. These and other "safe leaders" from among the business community and clergy had ties to liberal and progressive whites to whom they turned for fund raising and other support. These were also the men and women who organized and led such black organizations as the NAACP, the Urban League, the "colored" YWCA and YMCA, and other self-help organizations. Theirs was a moderate orientation, satisfied with a gradualist approach through an appeal to the goodwill and reason of whites.

During the Depression, however, some younger members of the middle class became more radical and introduced the boycott as a technique to force white merchants to hire blacks. When Communists became active in the black community, black middle-class leaders were soon replaced by more radical leaders or adapted their style to include boycotts, marches, and peaceful demonstrations. Eventually, as the Second World War made clear the contradictions of a fight for democracy overseas while maintaining racial inequality at home and in the armed forces, sentiments shifted from an emphasis on small gains and concessions to a demand for total equality. Throughout this process, it was the black middle class that provided the leadership, the tactical connections with cooperating whites, and the pressures (often accompanied by the implied threat of the leadership of more radical blacks or of violence from the masses) for change and for equality. The developing cracks in the walls of segregation during the 1940s and 1950s—the lowering of the job ceiling, integration in the armed forces, increased integration in civilian life in the North, and growth in the number of black college graduates and college students—proved to be just the beginning of an irresistible force that was to burst onto the American scene in the 1960s and profoundly alter the position of blacks in the United States. In the process, the conditions for the emergence of a *new* black middle class were created. It is to this latter development that I will turn in the next chapter.

# 2

# The New Black Middle Class: Has Race Been Eclipsed?

Much of the uniqueness of the old black middle class consisted in its emergence and way of life within a segregated society. This was especially true of blacks in the South; but even in the North, as has been demonstrated, middle-class blacks were frequently subjected to many of the same exclusionary practices, the same indignities, and the same marginality experienced by blacks in the South. As has also been pointed out, these conditions greatly distorted the composition of the black middle class, so that the largest stratum within the white middle class—clerical and sales workers—was the slowest to develop among blacks. Blocked in their attempts to compete for a broad range of middle-class occupations for the most part, during the first half-century blacks had to settle for those occupations serving the needs of growing black urban communities. This remained true up to the early 1960s, with a few "firsts" and "onlys"—a judge here, an engineer there—being exceptions to the rule rather than the beginning of a new trend of enlarged opportunities. By 1960, only 13 percent of all black workers held middle-class jobs, compared to 44 percent of all whites (fig. 4). In spite of efforts, which had begun during World War II, by the

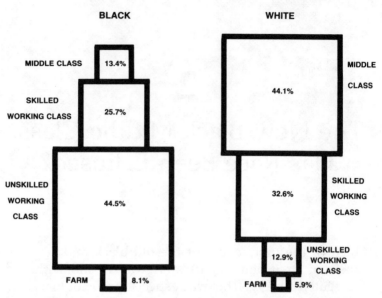

Fig. 4. Black and white class structures in 1960. *Sums do not equal 100.0 because of those for whom no occupation was reported.

Urban League and other groups to persuade white department stores in the North to hire black clerks, relatively few had been hired.

Nationally, only one out of ten black female workers had penetrated the clerical field. Though the proportion was higher in cities of the North—one-fourth in cities like Chicago—this was still a far cry from the more than 50 percent of white women with clerical and sales jobs. Nor were the sons of black middle-class parents more successful in capitalizing on their origins to *remain* in the middle class. In a national study of the occupational mobility of black and white males in 1962, Duncan concluded:

> Negro men who originated at the lower levels were likely to remain there; white men were likely to move

up. Negro men who originated at higher levels were likely to move down; white men were likely to stay there.[1]

In 1962, black males continued to find few job openings above the semiskilled blue-collar level. And many with a college degree found that even a diploma would not open the right doors. Those who did manage to enter the professional stratum continued to be barred from the major professional organizations and thus had to continue to maintain their own parallel groups. The fact is that at the beginning of the 1960s, despite local pressures by black organizations to open up new job categories and the enactment by some twenty states of Fair Employment Practices laws, the job ceiling remained very low—below the skilled blue-collar level for both males and females. For example, a survey in 1961 by the Bureau of Jewish Employment Problems of Chicago found that "98 per cent of the white collar job orders received from over 5,000 companies were not available to qualified Negroes."[2] For most middle-class jobs other than the ones blacks had traditionally been allowed to enter, black college graduates continued to encounter the invisible sign: "No Negroes Need Apply." As a result, most continued to pursue degrees in the traditional fields, especially education.

Black entrepreneurs continued to struggle, with only a few achieving notable success in publishing, insurance, or the manufacturing of cosmetics. With rare exceptions, talk of making inroads into the "American" market remained wishful thinking, as black businessmen had to continue their dependency on black consumers in the ghetto for virtually all their sales. Already faced with the fact that the bulk of the Negro market's money went to white downtown department stores and supermarkets, many viewed the slow development of integration with concern for their survival. This situation might have continued indefinitely had it not been for the development of two *simultaneous* and powerful forces within American society: prosperity and the civil rights movement. The chance simultaneous occurrence of these two factors, I will argue, created the necessary conditions for the emergence of a new black middle class.

## A NEW BLACK MIDDLE CLASS
## REPLACES THE OLD

Between 1960 and 1970 the percentage of middle-class blacks suddenly doubled, growing from about 1 in 8 to 1 out of every 4 black workers. While this was far below the 1 out of 2 level of whites in 1970, the gain experienced by the black middle class during the 1960s exceeded their total increase during the previous fifty years. It was a growth shared by both black men and black women in all three strata of the middle class: professionals, managers and small businessmen, and clerical and sales workers. Altogether, black males increased their representation in the middle class by 9 percent and black females by 17 percent, with most of their growth taking place at the clerical and sales level. The overall pattern of black middle class development had finally come to resemble that of whites, with the clerical stratum well ahead of the two others in size. However, growth in size is not sufficient reason to speak of a *new* black middle class. In what important ways did the black middle class in 1970 differ from the black middle class ten years earlier and in previous decades? And what brought about this change? I will first discuss the forces behind these statistical changes, then turn to an examination of differences between the old and new black middle class.

## MONTGOMERY: THE NEW JERICHO

From the time of slavery, black people have been fond of using the language of the Bible to describe their condition in the United States. From this perspective, the 1954 bus boycott in Montgomery, Alabama, was the beginning of a movement that would soon bring the walls of segregation tumbling down. It was a movement begun when a tired black maid, Rosa Parks, refused to take the accustomed extra steps to the back of the bus to make room for a white man. Without aiming to be a hero, she had started a revolution. By the early 1960s the movement had picked up momentum, with attention now having shifted from Montgomery to the more general issue of discrimination in public accommodations throughout the South. The decades, the years, of having to drive nonstop across the South because no hotels would accept them, the decades of sitting in the back of the bus, of drinking at "colored only" fountains of waiting in the back room of white doctors' offices, of segregated waiting rooms at bus and train terminals, of the long climb up dimly lit stairs to the balcony of theaters, of back-door and side-door entrances, and of waiting to be served until all white patrons had been taken care of had finally become unbearable. The Montgomery bus boycott had been led by a young, middle-class minister, Martin Luther King, Jr., but was sustained by poor blacks of the city, domestics, garbage collectors, and unskilled laborers as well as blacks of other classes. The new wave of protest in the early 1960s was now being led by the sons and daughters of the old middle class and by many who were moving up the class ladder, by students of the traditionally black colleges of the

South, by ministers and other middle-class organizers. It was a middle-class movement, and as some have criticized, it was at first a movement with middle-class goals—desegregation of public accommodations, many of which the masses of black poor could not hope to enjoy because of their poverty. In time, its goals were broadened to include equal access to jobs and the ballot box.

These middle-class ministers and students were soon joined by sympathetic blacks and whites from the North. With newly developed tactics inspired by Gandhi, nonviolent resistance was translated into the context of the Old South, and the movement soon captured sympathetic headlines and widespread support in the North. Sit-ins at segregated lunch counters, marches, freedom rides, and nonviolent resistance filled jails with middle-class protesters. In contrast to the *defensive* measures of the old black middle class in previous decades, an *offensive* effort now reigned. And it was a movement that at last could not be stopped by dogs, billy clubs, cattle prods, the Klu Klux Klan, or even death. It was a movement that finally bore fruit in the civil rights legislation of the mid-1960s. Fortunately, these laws did more than put an end to segregation at lunch counters, restaurants, and hotels; they also made discrimination in employment based on race a crime. And it was these new laws mandating equal employment opportunities that had the most far-reaching consequences for black people as a whole and that directly contributed to the growth of the new black middle class. This new legislation and the Equal Employment Opportunity Commission created to implement the law eventually brought access to a greater range of white collar jobs than ever available in the past. It is partly these enlarged opportunities for employment that leads me to refer to the black middle class by 1970 as a new black middle class.

## GROWTH FORMULA: PROSPERITY AND
## THE CIVIL RIGHTS MOVEMENT

Though it has become fashionable to attribute black economic gains in the 1960s to the civil rights movement, an examination of the 1950s and 1970s indicates that it was not a sufficient cause. The uniqueness of the 1960s lay in the fact that prosperity *and* the civil rights movement, culminating in equal employment opportunity laws, coincided. This was not the case during the 1950s or the 1970s.

There is no doubt that the decade of the 1950s was a period of prosperity. Recovery from the Depression was now complete, so much so that we were able to commit billions of dollars to rebuilding a devastated Europe. With our gross national product increasing at an annual rate of 3.2 percent, inflation running at only 2.1 percent, and an ever-expanding and vigorous economy, unemployment rates remained low, falling below 4 percent in six out of ten years among whites and only rising above 10 percent for blacks in the last two years of the decade. Reflecting both the full employment of that decade and increased productivity, median white family income rose by 41 percent between 1950 and 1959, from $7,057 to $9,970, and its middle class continued steady expansion from 40 to 44 percent. Even the earnings of blue-collar workers increased sharply during this decade—increasing even more rapidly than those of some segments of white-collar employees. Both the business community and social scientists reacted enthusiastically to these developments. *Fortune* magazine published a book entitled *The Changing American Market*, which spoke of a new "middle market" of affluent consumers.[3] And some social scientists proclaimed the total demise of classes in the United States. Chief among these spokesmen was Kurt Mayer, who wrote a series of articles from the mid-1950s to the early 1960s developing the idea that "the continuous expansion and mechanization of the American economy" was "now about to re-convert a substantial part of the working class into a brand-new middle class stratum."[4] Mayer went so far as to claim that because of a supposed increasing rate of mobility, the middle class was "well on the way to losing its class character altogether."[5] And many other scholars agreed with his position. We had become, in John Kenneth Galbraith's words, "the Affluent Society." Few challenged his optimism. Those who did so by writing about a ruling class, such as C. Wright Mills in the 1950s[6] and G. Williams Domhoff in the 1960s,[7] found far fewer readers than Galbraith's *Affluent Society*.[8]

Though blacks shared in the prosperity of the 1950s in terms of lower unemployment and higher incomes, the black middle class grew by only 3 percent, from 10 to 13 percent, with most of this gain occurring at the clerical level. The prosperity of the 1950s had contributed little to increasing the rate of black upward mobility into the middle class. Why? Because discrimination—including employment discrimination—was still the norm in both the North and the South, and there was nothing to force white employers to include blacks in the general prosperity by giving them equal access to the growing number of white-collar jobs. Prosperity alone was insufficient for the black middle class to grow beyond the 2 to 3 percent rate of previous decades.

If the 1950s demonstrated the futility of prosperity without laws mandating equal employment for the growth of the black middle class, the 1970s revealed the insufficiency of laws without prosperity. The deep recession of 1974–75 combined with high inflation, rising unemployment rates, which fell below 5 percent for whites in only two years of the decade, then recurrent recessions and double-digit inflation sent the economy into a slump, ending two decades of booming prosperity. Though equal employment opportunity laws remained on the books and the Equal Employment Opportunity Commission continued its enforcement efforts, the growth of the black middle class slowed dramatically. It is clear, then, that the most radical changes in black social structure came in the only decade to combine prosperity and legal incentives—the 1960s. During this period, as I pointed out earlier, both black males and black females significantly increased their representation in the middle class.

Between 1970 and 1980, however, black middle class growth again slowed, especially among black males, who increased their presence in the middle class by less than 1 percent. Almost all of the growth in the black middle class during this decade resulted from the ability of black women to continue finding white-collar jobs, particularly at the clerical level where demand was high. Their growth rate among professionals, however, declined by two-thirds, and their proportion decreased by 1 percent in the stratum of proprietors, and managers. Without prosperity, the civil rights laws lost much of their impact. Why?

## THE 1960s RECONSIDERED

Certainly, the reason for this loss of impact was not the unavailability of jobs. Though the growth of the white-collar sector slowed appreciably during the 1970s, both white males and females *increased* their proportions in the professional stratum by 2 percent. And unlike black females, white female representation at the level of proprietors and managers grew by almost 3 percent. Though white females, like black females, experienced a higher rate of upward mobility into the middle class than males, white females moved into higher-paying and higher prestige jobs than black females. Black females moved primarily into the clerical stratum, white females into the professional and managerial strata. While fewer than in the 1960s, jobs did exist in the 1970s. But blacks were no longer getting their fair share as they did in the 1960s. With fewer jobs available, white resistance to equal employment opportunity for blacks increased, eventually prompting cries of reverse discrimination and opposition to the successful techniques of quotas and timetables.

Comparisons with the 1950s and 1970s throw a new light on the black experience in the 1960s and the reasons for the development of a new black middle class. According to this analysis, the emergence of the new black middle class required *both* new laws giving blacks greater access to a wider range of middle-class occupations than had historically been the case *and* the existence of a larger pool of such jobs created by an economic boom. The first condition resulted from the civil rights movement, mandating the lifting of the color bar from the blue-collar to white-collar level. The second created the conditions for white acquiescence with, and even active support by, many for this *new definition* of equal opportunity—a definition that involved active government intervention into the process to ensure a more equitable outcome. And why not? With an ever-increasing supply of white-collar jobs, there were enough for blacks to be included without depriving whites.

Consider the economic facts of the 1960s, when the economy performed even more impressively than in the 1950s. The gross national product rose at an annual rate of 3.9 percent compared to 3.2 in the 1950s, and unemployment, though higher than in the 1950s, remained relatively low. This was especially true from 1966 to 1969 when the unemployment rate for whites remained below 3.5 percent and for blacks, below 7.5 percent. But even earlier, the unemployment rate for

white workers was below 5 percent in four out of the
first six years of the decade. White median family income, while growing somewhat more slowly than in
the 1950s, nevertheless increased by 36 percent. The
median for blacks and other nonwhites jumped by 55
percent, compared to 40 percent in the 1950s. Inflation,
the great eroder of income gains, averaged a mere 2.7
percent between 1960 and 1970. Even this average is
deceptive, since the first half of the decade saw inflation
rates of 1.7 percent or less. Not until the last three years
of the decade did inflation exceed 4 percent.

At the social and political levels, this period of expansion and prosperity gave rise to a new spirit of fairness
and generosity. Blacks, long short-changed politically,
socially, and economically, found a large proportion
of white Americans responding positively and sup-
portively to their demands for inclusion. Many whites
went so far as to join the struggle on picket lines,
marches, and demonstrations. Public opinion crystal-
lized in favor of a spate of new legislation supportive
of civil rights for black Americans, equal access to public accommodations, and equal employment opportunities—a revolution in values equal to those which gave
women the franchise in the 1920s and to the 1954
Supreme Court decision outlawing the separate but
equal doctrine. Among all the issues pushed by blacks
during the 1960s, equal access to the ballot box and to
jobs were probably the most significant and far-reaching. The vote brought potential political power, which
later was to bear fruit in a tremendous increase in the
number of black elected officials who would eventually
take the leadership of the new black middle class. Increased employment opportunity in a climate of white
support for black upward mobility—especially that occurring at the white-collar level—made possible the
most rapid expansion of the black middle class ever to
occur in a single decade up to that time, perhaps ever.

In comparison to previous periods of black economic progress, then, the uniqueness of the 1960s lay in the opportunities it offered large numbers of blacks to move into the upper levels of the occupational structure—white-collar employment. Earlier occupational gains during the 1920s and 1940s were primarily at the blue-collar level of unskilled and semiskilled work. Now black workers were at last getting a fairer share of the good, clean, front-office jobs, the professional, managerial, sales, and clerical jobs that command higher salaries, greater job security, and greater opportunities for advancement than those lower in the class structure.

## THE NEW VERSUS THE OLD BLACK MIDDLE CLASS: IS THE NEW BLACK MIDDLE CLASS REALLY NEW?

By 1970, a new normative climate in the area of race relations had emerged in the United States—in the South as well as the North. Black children born from this time on would know the brutality and fear of Jim Crow years only through history books and the stories told by parents and grandparents. It is this new climate together with increased occupational opportunities that were the underpinnings of the new black middle class. In the Old South of the 1950s, 1960s, and earlier, segregation in every aspect of life was the norm. Within this segregated world, blacks were forced to live. In the words of a woman in her forties, from a small Florida city, life was "a question of surviving, of adapting to, and of living with." It was a world in which blacks—including middle-class blacks—"knew their place" and lived daily within these restrictions. Because of the rigidity of segregation and the certainty of reprisals against those who dared violate the norms in any way, most blacks were able to shelter themselves from many indignities by living in their own world. The same woman who spoke of life in a small Florida town as a matter of surviving could not remember having ever been called "nigger" while growing up, because—as she explained—her parents made sure that she and her siblings knew and observed the norms of segregation. Everyone knew, and even had a story to prove, that "bad niggers"—those who dared a flagrant violation of southern mores—did not live long.

While blacks of all classes kept to themselves during the 1930s, 1940s, and 1950s, middle-class blacks especially were diligent in avoiding situations that reminded them of the dilemma of their status. Not only would they not attempt to have dinner at white restaurants downtown, they eschewed alike movies in the segregated balconies of white theaters and the substandard black theaters, preferring parties and dinners at home. In this context, a home assumed greater importance among blacks than whites. It was the symbol of success in a society that allowed them precious few opportunities for conspicuous achievement, and it was an oasis in a hostile environment. Behind closed doors, middle-class blacks could act as though the outside world that rejected them did not exist or at least could feel a little sheltered from it. As befitting their symbolic importance, homes were furnished as lavishly as possible, often well beyond the occupants' economic means.

Frazier argued that the black middle class "created a world of make-believe to shield itself from the harsh economic and social realities of American life."[9] It was a world in which middle-class blacks played at having a "society," a world in which *status* became an overriding value leading to conspicuous consumption, especially in clothes and automobiles. In the North, where blacks were beginning to work side-by-side with whites in offices and in schools, Frazier noted that whites were often surprised at the wardrobes of their black colleagues, wardrobes they themselves could not afford. The reason for this extravagance, he held, came from the black middle class's emulation of the life style of upper-middle-class and even upper-class whites. It was the triumph of style over substance.

While some have taken exception with Frazier's portrayal of the old black middle class's life style, it should be pointed out that Drake and Cayton came to much the same conclusion in their well-documented study of blacks in Chicago in the 1940s. Using expressions such as the "cult of clothes," "conspicuous consumption," and "society," they provided an even more detailed and convincing description of the "world of make-believe" that Frazier only sketched. And when examining black middle-class life in Chicago in 1961, sixteen years after their original study, they were prompted to write:

> Middle-class "society" is much as it was sixteen years ago. The same "clubs which set the pattern" when *Black Metropolis* was originally written are still "going strong." . . . Prosperity has made possible an extreme elaboration of the "cult of clothes" which serves to integrate the world of "society" and the world of the Church in upper-class and middle-class circles. Style shows and fashion revues are a fixture of the Bronzeville subculture, and no one sees anything incongruous about the guild of a Catholic church sponsoring a "Pert and Pretty Fashion Show," or a Baptist church presenting "Excelsiors in Fashion Review" at its thirty-third anniversary services.[10]

Some of this life style of the old black middle class, as we shall see in a later chapter, was taken over by the new black middle class. From an economic point of view, it can be argued that the years of living in a segregated world distorted the consumption "tastes" of middle-class blacks to such an extent that their preferences remain different from middle-class whites in many areas up to the present.

In spite of the protection gained by living in a separate world, middle-class blacks could not completely avoid the indignities of discrimination. They too had to sit at the back of the bus and use "colored only" waiting rooms at the bus station. They too had to wait patiently, without showing any displeasure, while whites who arrived after them were served. In the South, middle-class black women had to buy dresses without being able to try them on in some stores or had to have their clothes made by a black seamstress. And middle-class black children who wanted an ice cream cone were forced to stand at a designated spot at the lunch counter, then leave immediately upon being served. Even those who "enjoyed" the confidence of upper-class whites as "trusted Negroes" and "leaders" within the colored community found that their position of trust did not earn them an invitation to white homes or a seat at the front of the bus. For whites to invite even middle-class blacks to their homes or to dare to treat them as equals violated southern norms and brought on the risk of being dubbed "nigger lovers."

The North differed, as Drake and Cayton emphasized, not in the absence of segregation and discrimination but in its uncertainty. There, too, blacks often found themselves excluded from theaters and restaurants or faced the prospect of being ignored or kept waiting an inordinate length of time. One of the most difficult aspects of life in the North for middle-class blacks was the uncertainty of not knowing whether they were experiencing discrimination or the "normal" inefficiencies of lazy clerks and bureaucrats. It was this uncertainty that led most middle-class blacks even in the North to live in a separate world of their own and to venture out only occasionally to use facilities whites took for granted.

It should not be surprising, then, that it was this restrictive and demeaning aspect of black life that was the first target of the civil rights movement. While not being able to get a job as an engineer was difficult enough to live with, colored-only water fountains and being ignored at downtown stores was an even greater indignity that made one feel somehow subhuman. As the civil rights movement gained momentum in the early 1960s and there developed for the first time hope of eliminating these insults from their lives, many middle-class blacks were willing to brave cattle prods and snapping dogs in Selma, Birmingham, and elsewhere in the South. And as these incidents were beamed daily into every living room of the North through the electronic media, it became a happening that shocked the sensibilities of millions of whites who would not otherwise have taken two seconds to think about race relations. Slowly, a realization of the absurdity of this system, which Myrdal called "the American Dilemma," began to sink in. And with this awakening came a change in the normative climate of a North that became supportive of legislation to outlaw such indignities and create a new system committed to treating all Americans as equals. The immediate effect of the civil rights movement, then, was the elimination of the old system of segregation in public accommodations.

It was, at the same time, instrumental in the development of a new normative climate. While the way of life in the South and much of the North held the *expectation* that blacks would be kept in their place, segregated from the normal affairs of much of white society, the new laws clearly rendered these expectations illegal. Those attempting to continue these racist practices no longer had the weight of the legal system on their side and now ran the uncertain risk of being found in violation of the law of the land. This was something new for the South. It emboldened blacks almost everywhere to test their newly defined rights and tempered the response of whites. The system changed slowly, to be sure, and many ingenious ruses as well as outright acts of intimidation and violence were used by whites to resist the new order. There was, for instance, the restaurant in one small city in Louisiana which developed the practice of placing reserved signs at every table. When blacks came to the restaurant for dinner they were always told that all tables had been previously reserved. And there was the stubborn refusal of a gas station owner in Jackson, Mississippi, to comply, continuing to maintain "colored" and "white" rest rooms. As late as 1966 when driving through that city, I was directed to the "colored" rest room when I stopped for gas.

In time, however, the force of the new laws and the determination of blacks everywhere led to the emergence of a new normative climate in which the would-be discriminator rather than blacks were placed on the defensive. Whites, South as well as North, who discriminated became "racist" rather than regular guys, and those who attempted to block the access of blacks could no longer count on success, instead running the risk of losing face rather than being heroes. Particularly in the cities, the presence of blacks in restaurants, hotels, and the classrooms of formerly white universities gradually became commonplace. And so, contrary to the arguments of the Social Darwinists of the time, mores changed as a result of legislation.[11]

Those in the best position to take advantage of these newly defined rights were, of course, the black middle class. They were the only blacks with the economic resources to occasionally go to a downtown restaurant or stop at a motel or hotel while traveling through southern states. When Drake and Cayton took a second look at Chicago in 1961, they found that little had changed in the cultural and social life of middle-class blacks except that now some of their social events were held at previously segregated downtown hotels and restaurants, a trend that continued and eventually had a profound effect on the parallel institutional life that middle-class blacks had developed during the previous hundred years of segregation.

But if the life style of middle-class blacks did not immediately change, their *life chances* did. If we think of life chances as the consumption of necessary goods and services (such as education, health care, and housing) made possible by an individual's or family's economic resources, then there arose among middle-class blacks for the first time the possibility that their life chances would be determined by the size of their pocketbooks rather than the color of their skin. Now middle-class blacks could legally consume the same kinds and quality of goods and services as middle-class whites of the same economic means. Prior to the 1960s, middle-class blacks faced the frustration of being blocked in the consumption of many goods and services that they could afford. It did not matter if they could pay for a meal at a fine restaurant. The refusal of restaurants in the South to serve them or the fear of exposing themselves to insult in the North kept them away. Nor did comparable black restaurants emerge in the black community as a substitute, though attempts were made. Likewise, it did not matter if they could afford to send their children to the best colleges of the South, since admission was unthinkable.

As a result of the civil rights movement and the laws that were enacted in 1964, middle-class blacks now lived in a radically altered environment, an environment in which the normative climate mandated equal treatment rather than discrimination. There were no longer the same expectations of discrimination regardless of occupational and economic achievement. It was this dilemma—material success as defined by the American dream without the resulting benefits enjoyed by middle-class whites—that led to the feeling of marginality and even inferiority among blacks. And it was one of the major differences between the old and new black middle class. Now that dilemma had been eliminated, at least on paper, and the edge taken off the harsher aspects of being middle class but black. This difference alone would be enough to justify speaking of a *new* black middle class. But it fortunately did not stop there.

The mood of the mid-1960s was expansive and generous, and the consciousness of past and present injustice was keen. So when the Civil Rights Act was passed in 1964, Title VII mandating equal employment opportunity was included. Blacks were being given equal access not only to restaurants, lunch counters, and hotels but to jobs. It was this part of the Civil Rights Act, Title VII, together with the economic expansion of the 1960s that accounted for a dramatic increase in black upward mobility, an expansion in the variety of occupations held by middle-class blacks, and a sharp growth in the size of the black middle class by 1970.

## FROM WORKING CLASS TO MIDDLE CLASS: THE AMERICAN DREAM AWAKENS AND LIVES A LITTLE

As late as 1962, as we already saw, few of the sons and daughters of middle-class blacks managed to remain in that class, and even fewer from the working class moved up. It was not that middle-class jobs did not exist. The steady growth of the white middle class from 24 percent of the white labor force in 1910 to 44 percent in 1960 proves that they did—only not for blacks. Nor was it that upward mobility was not occurring among blacks at the beginning of the 1960s and earlier. Fifty-four percent of black males were in class positions higher than their fathers in 1962. But these had primarily been moves from farm to unskilled, working-class jobs or from farm and unskilled to semiskilled jobs in the working class. Only 1 in 5 of all black males who moved up in 1962 moved into the middle class, compared to more than 1 out of every 2 white males.

Now, for the first time, a law, Title VII of the Civil Rights Act, mandated that blacks be given equal access to these jobs. And while this was but the opening salvo of a battle that still rages, in the prosperous climate of the 1960s it had a measurable impact on black upward mobility. The new black middle class was one that now lived in a climate of greatly enhanced opportunities compared with those of the old middle class. By 1973, the proportion of upwardly mobile black males reaching the middle class had grown from 1 in 5 to 1 in 3. While still a far cry from the 58 percent of upwardly mobile white males moving into the middle class, it nevertheless far exceeded the expectations and experience of the old black middle class.

One of the results of this increased mobility into the middle class was that the black middle class in the mid-1970s was a class mainly "recruited" from the sons and daughters of garbage collectors, assembly line workers, domestics, waiters, taxicab drivers, and farmers. Even with the increased rate of inheritance within the middle class, around 80 percent of the black middle class is today first generation. This is true no less of the upper than the lower-middle-class stratum. Thus, with 40 and 23 percent of the black middle class having moved up from the skilled and unskilled strata of the working class, respectively, most of its members continue to have roots stretching far down into the neighborhoods and homes of truck drivers, assembly line workers, and waiters. As Frazier argued in the 1950s, because of its recency, the black middle class remains a class without its own unique traditions.

## Position Begins to Pay Off

The new climate in which the black middle class found
itself in the late 1960s and early 1970s was favorable not
only to increased opportunities to reach that class but
also to remain there. The inability to pass on its position
to its offspring that characterized the old black middle
class led Duncan to comment in 1962:

> From one point of view, the occupational mobility data
> suggest that the Negro family has lesser impact on its
> son's occupational chances than does the non-Negro
> family. . . . In this respect, the Negro occupational mo-
> bility pattern is a more "open" or "equalitarian" one,
> but it is an equality that consists in the sharing by all
> members of the race in a lack of access to skilled or
> prestigious occupations.[12]

By contrast, the new black middle class was one with
greatly enhanced opportunities, giving new meaning to
middle-class origins for blacks. Between 1962 and 1973,
the proportion of black males "inheriting" their middle-
class positions more than doubled, so that now almost
one out of every two with middle-class parents remained in the middle class. Sons of black professionals
were especially successful in either becoming professionals themselves by 1973 or of remaining in the middle
class by taking clerical or sales jobs in the lower middle
class—a marked improvement over work on the assembly line, which they would have had to settle for earlier.
While not so successful as upper-middle-class blacks in
transmitting their class position to their children, by the
late 1960s and early 1970s, an increasing number of the
children of black sales and clerical families either remained at that level or moved up to the professional
level. The association between the class position of black
parents and that of their children was strengthened,

therefore, at both levels of the black middle class. That association is, of course, the commonsense expectation of every American. Having reached the middle class, a family expects to be able to use the advantages of that position to successfully sponsor their children in the contest for middle-class careers. But it did not work that way for the old black middle class. The result was that only about 1 in 10 black middle-class males in 1962 came from the middle class, compared to 4 out of 10 whites.

## TEACHERS, PREACHERS, AND NOW A FEW ENGINEERS

Blacks moving into the middle class during the 1960s and 1970s also found a greater variety of career choices than in the past. There were not simply more white-collar jobs to be had, there was greater diversity. Unlike the old black middle class, which was restricted to serving the needs of blacks ignored by indifferent or even hostile white professionals, the new black middle class was becoming, like whites, a class of salaried white-collar workers. By the mid-1970s, this new black middle class was no longer confined to the few professional occupations of teacher, minister, doctor, dentist, lawyer, and social worker. A national sample of the black and white middle classes that I collected in 1976 turned up no less than 65 different job titles held by black males, including accountant, engineer, sales manager, policeman, scientist, and architect. More and more, middle-class blacks could be found working side by side with their white counterparts in the offices of government bureaucracies and private industry, although, as we shall see below, government—especially the federal government—has been far more receptive to hiring blacks in middle-class positions than private industry. Black women also were increasingly visible as secretaries in front offices, as clerks in downtown department stores, and as bank tellers. This decline in the concentration of middle-class blacks in a few traditional occupations serving blacks was taking place faster among black males than females and faster in the Northeast than in other regions.

About a quarter of black middle-class males in the above sample were found in seven occupations: social worker (3.3%), secondary schoolteacher (5.1%), elementary schoolteacher (2.3%), mail carrier (3.3%), postal clerk (5.1%), clerical supervisor (2.8%), and policeman (4.7%). Almost half of black middle-class wives, however, were concentrated in just six occupations, all traditional "female" occupations: registered nurse (9.9%), social worker (6.4%), elementary schoolteacher (14.6%), secondary schoolteacher (2.3%), retail sales clerk (5.3%), and secretary (8.8%). While white middle-class wives were also found primarily in traditional female areas, the majority were spread over nine rather than six occupations.

In past decades, before the civil rights laws mandated equal employment opportunities for blacks, Woodson and Frazier found that blacks had been able to enter the more lucrative and prestigious professional careers of medicine and law in greater numbers in the North. That greater opportunities historically found by blacks in the North continued even after Title VII of the Civil Rights Act could be seen in the larger variety of upper-middle-class occupations that black males were able to enter there: 41 compared to only 29 in the South and 28 in the North Central region.

It is in the rapid growth of the number of black clerical workers following the enactment of the civil rights laws, however, that we can observe one of the most striking differences between the old and new black middle class. In the old order, as we have seen, even in the North blacks were not hired in positions involving contact with a white public. No longer restricted to working in black businesses and colleges, black women in my 1976 sample were employed in more than twenty-three different clerical jobs, including jobs in banks, department stores, libraries, hotels, and the front offices of businesses. The result of Title VII was a 100 percent increase—from 10 to 22 percent—in the proportion of black women working in the clerical and sales fields between 1960 and 1970. In spite of less favorable economic conditions in the 1970s, black women continued to get a share of these jobs, and by 1976, one out of every four black women in the labor force was engaged in clerical or sales work, compared to one in ten in 1960. By the mid-1970s, also, the distribution of black middle-class workers had come to resemble the distribution of whites: a large stratum of clerical and sales workers, a smaller stratum of professionals, and an even smaller stratum of managers and small businessmen. As recently as 1960, when white clerical and sales workers outnumbered professionals by 100 percent, there were less than 3 percent more blacks in clerical and sales than in professional occupations.

## Black Businesses Wade into the Mainstream—a Little

Black businessmen, also, have fared better in this new climate, prompting the energetic Earl Greaves to begin publishing a business-oriented magazine, *Black Enterprise*, in 1970 "for black men and women who want to get ahead." In 1973, an article entitled "The Top 100 Black Businesses" appeared in its June issue. It has been an annual feature ever since. While many of these top 100 black-owned businesses such as cosmetics manufacturing, supermarkets, publishing, and real estate firms served an exclusive or predominantly black clientele, as in the past, in 1974 a number provided a service or product consumed by whites as well as blacks. Heading the list was Motown Industries, whose sales of records by Stevie Wonder, Marvin Gaye, Gladys Knight, and other top black entertainers to whites and blacks alike brought it a gross income of $46 million. Other black businesses reaching a general market included construction companies, equipment leasing firms, some automobile dealerships, and manufacturing firms. Manufacturing is especially noteworthy since it represents the area that black entrepreneurs have had the greatest difficulty entering. In addition to cosmetics and records, black manufacturers in 1974 were turning out sausage and pork products, electronic equipment, pharmaceutical products, metal products, containers, and janitorial equipment. Though in the minority among black businesses, black manufacturers represent progress from the days of the old black middle class when virtually all were small service-oriented businesses such as barbershops, beauty parlors, grocery stores, real estate dealers, and funeral parlors. All businesses included in *Black Enterprise's* top 100 in 1974 had gross sales between $1.6 million and $46 million, small, perhaps, when compared to those of whites but a substantial improvement over the past.

## WHAT HAS HAPPENED TO THE SIGNIFICANCE OF RACE?

I have argued that the black middle class emerging in the late 1960s and early 1970s following the upheavals of the civil rights movement and the laws enacted in 1964 is a *new* black middle class compared to the one preceding it. It is new because of the changed normative climate, a climate increasingly free of the violence, intimidation, indignities, and social restrictions of the past. This was a climate in which middle-class blacks increasingly had access to whatever services their money could buy rather than being locked out by the color of their skin. It is new, also, as a result of Title VII of the Civil Rights Act and prosperity, which increased access to a greater variety of middle-class jobs, creating a black middle class that differed significantly from the old in its composition. No longer did one automatically expect a member of the black middle class to be a teacher, a minister, a postal worker, or, perhaps, a doctor or lawyer. A black middle-class person might now be an engineer, an accountant, a consultant, a government bureaucrat, or maybe even a middle-range executive or elected official. For a variety of reasons, then, it was appropriate to speak of a new black middle class by 1970.

With many of the social restrictions of the past lifted and with increasing access to a wider variety of white-collar careers, what has happened to the important distinction of race? Has the significance of race disappeared or at least dramatically declined, as Wilson suggested?[13] Wilson's argument is not that racism has disappeared from the American scene altogether, however, but that it has declined in significance in the "economic" sector to such an extent that "economic class is now a more important factor than race in determining job placement"[14] and "black life-chances in the modern industrial period."[15] It is a conclusion based on recent changes in the economy that he holds—as have others—resulted in a segmented labor market. But Wilson goes considerably further than the others who postulate a segmented or dual labor market in that he sees this "resulting in vastly different mobility opportunities for different groups in the black population."[16] Other writers have tended to see a black-white division along segmented lines but not differing economic chances *within* the black population itself. As Wilson sees it, this economic segmentation among blacks has brought permanence to the positions of the *already existing* black underclass while—together with enacted civil rights laws—giving middle-class blacks the same opportunities as whites with similar qualifications.[17] It is quite a leap, however, from the recognition that the most blatant patterns of racial oppression and racial strife in the labor market have diminished substantially to the conclusions that now the position of the black underclass is perpetuated primarily by the impersonal forces of the market and that "talented and educated blacks are experiencing unprecedented job opportunities in the growing government and corporate sectors . . . that are *at least comparable* to those of whites with equivalent qualifications."[18] Wilson presents little or no solid data to support these assertions, which will be addressed in greater detail in chapter 8.

While this comparison of the old black middle class and the new black middle class might at first seem to support Wilson's argument, it makes the position of the latter appear more substantial than is actually the case because of the desperate situation of the former. This is not meant to diminish the real progress made. But the only true test of the position of the black middle class today is a detailed comparison with that of its counterpart, the white middle class. There cannot be two standards of success, one white, the other black. There is one standard against which both blacks and whites must be measured. That is why I have avoided the approach some writers have taken of defining the black middle class and the white middle class differently. Class is class; success is success.

Now that there is a new black middle class, the important question is how successful it is compared to the white middle class rather than to the old black middle class. It is this question that I will attempt to answer in the following chapters using extensive national interview and census data from the 1970s and 1980s.

# 3

# Moving On Up: At Last
# a Piece of the Pie

The 1960s produced a new normative climate for blacks
and created opportunities that enabled the new black
middle class to far outstrip its predecessor. But did this
place it within striking distance of the white middle
class? As a group, was the black middle class approach-
ing the white middle class in total size and in the distribution of its three principal strata: professionals, small
businessmen and managers, and sales and clerical
workers? As individuals, were blacks and whites following the same path into the middle class, and once there,
did they experience equivalent success? The answer is
still no. The experience of today's black middle class
remains separate and substantially different from that
of the white middle class.

## THE UPWARD CLIMB

The main stages of an individual's move up the class
ladder have become well known in recent years, beginning quite logically with family background, moving
through the educational system, and ending in the job
market. The model developed by sociologists to map

out this journey is quite simple. The father's occupation, or his occupation and education together, represents family background. The years of schooling completed measure educational attainment, and the first or current occupation represents success in the job market.[1] This model, with minor variations, has been successfully applied again and again to analyze the occupational achievement of white males but only infrequently that of blacks. When applied to black males, it becomes clear that it does not provide a good fit. In my own research, I found that the classic model explained far less about the experiences of black than of white males, especially in the beginning of their careers.[2] Studies of occupational attainment have usually explained the *general process* of moving up the occupational ladder rather than moves into a particular position. My concern is to understand how blacks have managed to move into a *particular* position, the middle class, and to determine whether they follow the same paths as whites. To do this, I have modified the basic model described above by considering some unique aspects of the family background of blacks.

The basic achievement model assumes that husband and wife play the traditional roles of breadwinner and nurturer-housewife, respectively. It also assumes that the husband's role is the most important aspect of family background influencing the achievement of children. This model oriented to the "successful male" fits the experience of whites far more than that of blacks. Although recent research has convincingly demonstrated that most black families have historically had a husband present,[3] it is equally true that black males have been considerably less successful in the competition for jobs and income. At the same time, significantly more black wives than white wives have historically taken on a share of the breadwinner role. Still other studies have pointed to the involvement of members of the extended family in the achievement process.[4] All of this suggests that understanding the drama of black middle-class achievement required a redefinition of familial roles peculiar to the black experience. Since black males have been less successful economically, for instance, we need to identify other sources of economic support that enable some blacks to reach the middle class. And if the educational level of white fathers has been successfully used to represent the socialization influencing high achievement, in view of the lower educational levels of black males, we want to discover what the sources of motivation are among blacks.

## STRIVING FAMILIES

To answer these questions, I examined a national sample of black and white males who had entered the middle class by 1976,[5] about ten years after the passage of Title VII of the Civil Rights Act. Even though the boom years of the 1960s had passed and the nation was struggling out of one of the deepest postwar recessions, these black and white males had already reached the middle class. The influences that helped them get there had already been played out and therefore could be studied in depth.

The black males had come in almost equal numbers from the unskilled working class, the skilled working class, and the middle class, with another 13 percent from farms. As the analysis of their upward journey into the middle class progressed, it became clear that their common experience was a beginning in what could only be called striving families. These were families that placed a high value on achievement and that drew on every available economic and emotional resource to help their children acquire the education that would open the door to the middle class. And when gaps appeared at some point in this effort, there was often assistance from kin and community. The struggle was greater for some families than for others, but, overall, it was evident that considerably more effort was needed for blacks to reach the middle class.

## Multiple Roles

The striving was first of all evident in the number of roles played by both fathers and mothers, and the difficulty involved in reaching the middle class was demonstrated by the greater number of factors that were present among blacks who went to college than among whites. Whether or not *white* males acquired sufficient education to qualify for middle-class jobs depended primarily on their father's class position and their parents' educational levels. These three factors (father's class, father's education, and mother's education) showed the closest association to the educational achievement of white sons when looked at individually and had the strongest *direct, causal* influence when examined together with a variety of other factors using a powerful statistical technique called path analysis.[6] Only in the case of large white families did the additional factor of mother's encouragement have a statistically significant effect; whether she worked had no impact on a son's educational achievement. As a group, in most families from which white middle-class males had come in 1976, the salaries of fathers were sufficiently high that their mothers did not have to work. This is not surprising, as half the middle-class whites had come from middle-class homes and another third from the skilled working class.

It was just the opposite among blacks who made it into the middle class: less than one-third came from middle-class homes, and a large percentage of the mothers had to work to supplement their husbands' low incomes. Evidence of the positive impact of black mothers' economic contribution on their sons' educational achievement can be found both in the higher educational achievement of sons of working mothers and in the direct causal link in the path model. Unlike white wives, black wives' additional economic role often enabled their sons and daughters to obtain a college education. In the mid-1980s, the high employment rate among wives of both races has become commonplace. The above findings reveal, however, that the employment of wives from economic necessity has been a pattern among blacks for several decades prior to the 1980s. While many black mothers were forced to add an economic role to their traditional role of nurturing, many black fathers added nurturing to their traditional role as breadwinner. The association between the educational achievement of middle-class males in the mid-1970s and their fathers' encouragement was stronger among blacks than among whites—almost as strong as the association between the encouragement of black mothers and their sons' education.

Whether black fathers encouraged their sons to high achievement often depended on their own educational level and the number of children in the family. The higher the educational level of black fathers, the likelier they were to actively encourage their sons to go beyond high school. In fact, the family influence most strongly associated with the educational achievement of middle-class black sons was the amount of education possessed by their fathers and mothers. The combined effect of the educational levels of black parents not only had a far stronger influence on their sons attending college than any other factor but also had a stronger influence among blacks than whites. Given that the *class position* of black fathers had little influence on the educational achievement of their sons, it would seem that whether or not black males (and females) acquired sufficient education to qualify them for middle-class jobs depended more on the degree to which they were encouraged by their fathers and mothers than on the material resources of the family. While this might seem strange at first, social scientists have long observed the greater emphasis blacks have placed on education compared to whites. In part, this emphasis came from the belief that education was the only key to occupational success in a society that discriminated on the basis of color. In part, also, a college degree has historically earned greater prestige within the black community than the white community because of the rarity of such an achievement among blacks. Black parents of all classes, then, encourage their children to strive for a college education as a means of pursuing the American dream of material and social success.

This conclusion is supported by the statistics showing that black middle-class males in 1976 came almost equally from the unskilled working class, the skilled working class, and the middle class (fig. 5). What was lacking in material resources among many of these families was compensated for by the level of motivation instilled in their children and the help of community members. This motivation is a sign of the type of culture developed in these striving families. The achievement of these middle-class sons was neither a chance occurrence nor the result of focusing all material and emotional resources on just one child. Almost half of these black middle-class males who completed college had at least one brother who had also gone to college. Nearly as many had sisters with some college education—quite an achievement for families with limited income. It was otherwise with those who had not made it into the middle class. Only one-fourth of black working-class males in my 1976 sample had a brother or sister who had attended college.

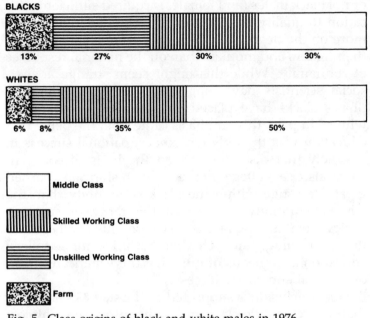

Fig. 5. Class origins of black and white males in 1976.

Responses to questions about educational funding revealed both the advantage of a middle-class background and the handicap of race. More blacks from middle-class than working-class homes listed their parents as the major source of financial support for college, but more often this depended on two wage earners. While the middle-class advantage represents the reality of class among blacks as well as whites, the need for two wage earners confirms the disadvantage experienced because of being black. This deficit was also observable in the greater financial support white males from both middle- and working-class homes received compared to blacks from similar homes. Blacks, especially those from working-class homes, were also more likely to have dropped out of college for financial reasons. The second and third most important sources of college financing for black males from middle-class homes were part-time work and scholarships. Those who moved up from skilled and unskilled working-class homes were more likely to have relied on scholarships first and parents second for their educational expenses. It should be noted that substantially more middle-class wives of both races reported receiving their primary educational support from parents. This was true regardless of class origin. Apparently, parental protectiveness of girls extends to educational support as well as other areas of life.

These striving families often had to overcome obstacles other than economic ones to enable their sons and daughters to gain a college education. Regardless of parental efforts, for instance, blacks living in the South and in small cities were less likely to acquire a college education than those in the North and in large cities. In addition, fewer older black males had attended college by 1976. For white middle-class males in 1976, however, neither region, nor size of place, nor age had any significant impact on the amount of education they had been able to acquire. The greater difficulty experienced by these black males results from impediments caused by segregation, which operated more severely in the past and which is still more likely to exist in the South and in small cities.

Three other factors were examined for their impact on the upward climb to the middle class: birth order, the number of children in a family, and whether or not both parents were present. These factors might be expected to influence an individual's chance to acquire a college education and enter the middle class for a number of reasons. The larger the number of children, the more thinly financial resources have to be spread among them and fewer are the resources available for any single child. Likewise, firstborn and only children tend to receive more attention and support than second or subsequent children. Finally, it has been generally assumed (though not proven) that children—particularly sons—coming from homes in which a father was not present experience lower achievement.[7]

Surprisingly, rigorous analysis of my 1976 data unearthed no direct negative effect of these three factors on the educational achievement of black males (even though having more than one child reduced the chance of white males gaining a college degree). Given the commonsense expectations noted above, how is this possible? It should be remembered that although relevant, economic resources did not always prevent—or ensure—educational achievement among blacks. An equal number of black males from each of the three classes above the farm class had managed to enter or remain in the middle class by 1976, most of them with at least some college education. The same was true for black middle-class wives. Just as important as material resources for educational achievement was their socialization. Those who acquired some college education came from families (large or small) that placed a high value on achievement and that *were able* to back this value with emotional and economic support. When families were large—and already strained economic resources thinned—emotional support was even more important. In those cases, black fathers, regardless of class, became more involved in the socialization of their children and in encouraging them to pursue a college education. In view of the discrimination faced by black youth, parental encouragement and support was more important than among whites and had a direct and positive effect on their educational achievement. This involvement of black fathers seems to have compensated somewhat for the thinning out of resources in a large family, thus diminishing the negative effect of meager resources on educational achievement. No such relationship between the size of family and father's encouragement was discovered among whites, and the more children in the family, the less white mothers were likely to be involved in their sons' socialization.

One out of five middle-class black males in my sample came from homes in which the father was absent while they were growing up and yet managed to attend college and reach the middle class. While this achievement attests to the effectiveness of many single mothers, it was also in part a result of the interest taken in them by teachers, relatives, ministers, and other members of the community. Analysis revealed that community members and relatives were most likely to become involved in encouraging those who made it into the middle class when there was no father present. Often, this made the difference between attending college and later obtaining a middle-class job and an education that ended with high school. Community members and relatives were also more likely to support sons other than the firstborn or an only child. Thus, the difficulty created by an absent father or by a large family was often overcome through the interest of community members or relatives.

This first stage in the journey to the middle class (family background) emerges as a very complicated one for blacks, one in which the possibility of acquiring a college education is conditional on eight factors compared to only four among whites. At this stage, black mothers have frequently had to add an economic role to supplement the low incomes of black fathers. At the same time, black fathers and community members have had to become more involved in the socialization process to counteract the negative effects of large families, low incomes, and absent fathers. In spite of their efforts, blacks living in the South and in small cities and older blacks were less likely to earn a college degree than their counterparts who lived in the North or in large cities or who were younger. Those whites who reached the middle class, however, found the journey comparatively less problematic, with parents playing traditional roles and with no need for community involvement.

## The Importance of a College Education

The significance of the second stage in the journey to the middle class—acquiring a college education—cannot be overstated. Unlike the early 1960s, by the mid-1970s few blacks with a college education had failed to make it into the middle class; relatively few (especially males) made it without some college education. This was true regardless of family origin. Eighty percent of black males and 60 percent of black females from middle-class families who *remained* in the middle class had attended college. Most of those who experienced downward mobility either had not attended college or had not earned a degree. Of those who had *moved upward* into the middle class from the skilled and unskilled strata of the working class by 1976, over half the males and nearly half their wives either had a college degree or had attended college for a number of years. Education was at last beginning to pay off for blacks—if it could be acquired.

The importance of a college education for reaching the middle class should not be surprising given the requirements of most middle-class occupations. All professional occupations require a college diploma or advanced degree; the days of moving up from office boy to executive are long past. Businesses now recruit from among those who have earned an M.B.A. or an undergraduate business degree. Even most of those who start their own businesses today have some college education, a necessary asset given the intellectual demands of operating in the present competitive climate. Only within the clerical and sales stratum can we find a high percentage of workers without a college degree. This is the reason the number of college educated middle-class females is smaller than that of males. Many females are able to reach the middle class through clerical and sales jobs. But even in the clerical field, many workers have some college training or have at least attended a secretarial school beyond their high school education. For black (or white) families who want their children to remain in the middle class or move up to it, the task is clear: help them earn a college education so they can qualify for a middle-class occupation.

Although the analysis revealed that some family characteristics *directly* influence a son's or daughter's chance of obtaining a middle-class job when *entering* the labor market after school, this influence is far weaker than the influence of the amount of education possessed by the individual. Education is important in an individual's attempt to reach the middle class both as the single most significant *direct causal link* with occupation and as a transmitter of most family influences.

## THE HURDLE OF THE FIRST JOB

Despite education's role as the most important link to a middle-class occupation, significant differences were found in how education affected blacks and whites. Blacks had greater difficulty translating a college education into a middle-class job when first entering the labor force after school. In the past, this lower success rate of black college graduates was blamed on quality of education. Blacks, it was argued, attended predominantly black schools that provided an education inferior to that of schools attended by whites. Inferior education was then translated into lower job success. When subjected to rigorous statistical analysis, however, this assumption has been proven false. Duncan, for instance, has demonstrated that if the family background and education of blacks and whites were equalized, an income gap would nevertheless remain which can only be attributed to discrimination.[8] And in a study matching eight hundred black and white male graduates from the same college with similar backgrounds, Robert Althauser and Sydney Spivack found that whites consistently obtained better jobs and received higher incomes than blacks.[9] Again, these authors drew the unavoidable conclusion that the resulting income and occupational differences were attributable primarily to discrimination.

In my own sample, almost three-fourths of the college-educated black males and females had attended a predominantly white college, two-thirds of which were in the North or West. The greater difficulty blacks experience in translating their hard-earned college degree into a middle-class job after leaving school, then, does not come from inferior schooling; it comes from discrimination. The data also revealed that blacks in the North were more likely than those in the South to enter the middle class at the time of their *first* job. Since the South has historically discriminated more severely than the North, this is another indication that discrimination is a serious obstacle to the movement of blacks into the middle class. For blacks, the difficulty in acquiring a college degree is frequently followed by the frustration of not being able to find a job for which they have acquired the credentials. The college degree does not automatically open the door to the good life. To compound the problem, Althauser and Spivack found in their study of matched samples of black and white males that black college graduates earned an average of between $1,100 and $2,300 less than whites.[10] That this income gap widens with educational level further indicates that discrimination continues to exert its harm even for blacks within the middle class.

Although blacks have greater difficulty than whites

in converting a college education into a middle-class occupation when entering the labor force, the effect of education fortunately continues beyond the first job. In fact, among blacks, the influence of education on a male's chance to reach the middle class was stronger *later* in his career than in the beginning. This is in sharp contrast to white males, whose payoff for their college degrees in the beginning of their careers was equal to or stronger than their payoff later on.[11] It would seem, then, that in time black males make up some of the deficit experienced early in their careers. Since many of the men in this sample entered the labor force before the civil rights laws were enacted these latter gains may in part suggest that some older males with college degrees profited from Title VII by securing middle-class jobs in the late 1960s and the 1970s which were earlier withheld from them. It may be that because of discrimination and other intangibles such as "connections" that favor whites, blacks take longer than whites to convert their college credentials into the payoff of a middle-class career. Whatever the reasons, it is clear that entry-level occupations influence later class position less among black males than among white males. For blacks, education remains the single most important avenue into the middle class, even though the payoff may be lower and take longer.

Among blacks, reaching the middle class also depends more on the *direct* influence of family background than among whites. White males find that a middle-class career is directly conditional on some family background factors, but these factors are fewer and more "logical." College-educated white males in 1976 who were living in large cities or who were firstborn sons, for example, were more successful in securing middle-class jobs. Finding a middle-class job when first entering the labor force was directly conditional for black males on *five* family background factors: size of family, region of residence, the presence of a father when growing up, father's class position, and family educational level. Without attempting to explain the role of all of these factors, we can conclude that their conditioning influences reinforce the earlier impression of the greater complexity in the process of blacks reaching the middle class.

PLAYING CATCH-UP

What do these racial differences in the process of reaching the middle class mean for blacks as a group? While new black middle-class families were much more successful than the old in helping their children reach the middle class, racial differences linger. Black middle-class families continue to be less successful than whites. By 1976, only slightly more than one-half (58%) of all black males from middle-class families themselves maintained their middle-class position compared to over three-fourths (82%) of white males of the same origins. Even when we compare upwardly mobile blacks and whites from the working class, we find that although proportionally more blacks than whites moved upward in 1976, fewer actually crossed into the middle class. Translated to the group level, these racial differences mean that the proportion of white male workers who had reached the middle class by 1976 was *double* the proportion of blacks (21 to 44). Adding black females to these calculations raises the percentage of black workers with middle-class jobs to 31 percent, still far behind the 53 percent figure for white males and females—even though far more black females than white females work full-time.

Although the new black middle class has made great strides compared to the old, the greater difficulty blacks experience in successfully negotiating the journey to the middle class means that the size of the black middle class will lag behind that of the white middle class for decades to come. This would be true even if the most favorable mobility patterns and economic conditions from the late 1960s and early 1970s continued. But, as we have seen, by the mid-1970s deteriorating economic conditions had begun to decrease the pace of black mobility into the middle class, especially that of black males, further delaying the time when the black and the white middle class will be of equal size.

Beyond the issue of size is the distribution of blacks among the three major strata of the middle class: professionals, small businessmen and managers, and clerical and sales workers. I have already noted that by the early 1950s the black middle class had come to resemble the white middle class in the *relative* size of these strata. That is, among both groups, the clerical and sales workers were about equal in number to the combined strata of professionals and managers and small businessmen—a development brought about by civil rights legislation giving black women access to clerical and sales positions in white businesses. Nevertheless, in 1976, the size of each stratum still lagged far behind that of whites (fig. 6). Just how far behind becomes strikingly evident from the following comparisons. By 1976, black professionals comprised 10 percent of all black workers, a level whites had already exceeded by 2 percent in 1960. And the 18 percent level of black clerical and sales workers had been reached by whites more than four decades earlier, in 1930. Farthest behind was the stratum of black businessmen and managers whose share of the black labor market, 3.5 percent, in 1976 was not yet equal to the percentage of whites in that stratum in 1910. The degree to which the new black middle class lags behind in the managerial-entrepreneurial stratum is particularly significant since it is here that the middle class finds its greatest opportunities for the accumulation of wealth and the exercise of power and authority.

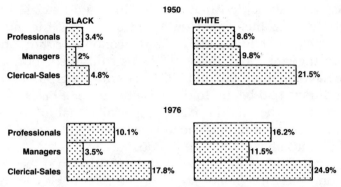

Fig. 6. Distribution of middle-class black and white workers by strata in 1950 and 1976 as percentage of total black and white labor forces.

## MALE-FEMALE CLASS DIFFERENCES

If we look separately at the distribution of males and females in the middle class, other important differences between blacks and whites appear. While among both blacks and whites a significantly higher proportion of females than males held middle-class jobs, the difference was greater among blacks. By 1976, nearly twice as many black females as black males were middle class; among whites, females outnumbered males only one and one-half times. Though this predominance of women in the middle class was largely a result of their near-monopoly of clerical and sales jobs within both races, there was also almost twice the percentage of black female professionals as male. Among whites, we find the same proportions of males and females in the professional stratum (fig. 7).

Black males also had a smaller edge than white males in the "male stratum" of managers and small businessmen, exceeding the percentage of females by only about one and two-thirds compared to two and one-half times for white males. Although representing percen-

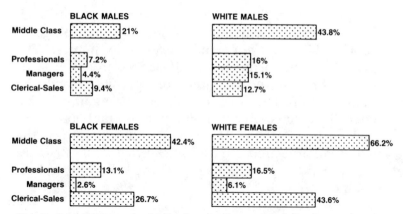

Fig. 7. Distribution of middle-class males and females by race and strata in 1976 as percentage of total black and white labor forces.

tages of workers rather than absolute numbers, these statistics still point to the greater difficulty black males experience in penetrating traditionally male occupations in the middle class, such as engineering, accounting, management, and other fields not historically open to blacks. The greater success of black females is more a result of their concentration in traditionally black professions such as teaching and social work than their entrance into traditionally male fields. As we will see in the following chapter and in chapter 8, black females attempting to enter the middle class, or already there, suffer the double discrimination of being black and female. It is discrimination that can be observed from both occupational and income statistics.

## THE TARNISHED SUCCESS
## OF LIFE IN THE MIDDLE

From time to time, articles about the black middle class appear in the press. Punctuated with code words of achievement such as "aristocracy," "old black society,"

and, especially, "black elite," these articles picture smil-
ing, successful-looking blacks amid the trappings of
comfortable and apparently expensive homes. The
group's accomplishments are described in enthusiastic
terms through the examples of specific individuals.
They are depicted as confident, possessing impeccable
educational credentials, holding important jobs, and
making large salaries. Typical of such articles was the
one that appeared in the *Washington Post Magazine*
on January 4, 1981. It began in the following upbeat
manner:

> In April 1979 a few black graduates of Harvard Law
> School held an after-work cocktail party for the other
> black alumni of "The Law School" working in Wash-
> ington. They thought there were enough alumni here
> to have a small affair. *Surprise:* One hundred people
> showed up.[12]

Like the men and women described in a *Washingtonian
Magazine* article, "Washington's Other Elite," in May
1982, these young professionals were viewed as successful measured on an "absolute yardstick" rather than by
black standards. Now they could increasingly be found
in the best places. "To walk K Street at noon in 1981,"
the writer boasted, "is to see black faces in the best suits
and dresses, at the best restaurants, entering the most
glamorous office buildings."[13]

Without a doubt, these articles describe real people
who have made it in a white world. But scratch the
surface and another reality appears. Like the old black
middle class that preceded them, these young members
of the new black middle class find all too often that
though the racial climate has greatly improved, it is still
not color blind—as another *Washington Post* article, "The
New Insensitivity," demonstrated. Written just a few
months after the *Washington Post Magazine's* "The Black

Elite," this article described the racial slurs and embarrassing moments middle-class blacks experience because of lingering racism. These episodes range from outright insulting remarks directed at blacks to remarks stemming from persistent stereotypes. In the former category, there is no doubt about the intentions and feelings of the whites involved; they are racists who direct their negative feelings at blacks when least expected. In one such case, a group of blacks in a New York City wine bar overheard nearby white patrons making racial slurs, one finally saying to another in a loud voice, "We treated them a lot better than a lot of other countries because we haven't eaten them." On another occasion, the daughter of Congressman Ronald Dellums (D, Calif.) was called a "coon" by a group of white boys outside a drugstore on fashionable Connecticut Avenue in Washington, D.C.[14]

Examples of embarrassment caused middle-class blacks by ingrained white racial stereotypes are also numerous. There was the incident, for example, when Rod Gaines, a vice president for TWA, was sitting in a Connecticut Avenue shoe store waiting to be served and a white woman approached him and asked, "Do you work in this area or the next?"[15] Another example comes from black writer Orde Coombs. On one occasion when depositing a large check from a publisher, Coombs was not sure of his account. When he asked a white cashier to check the number for him, she replied, "Did he tell you to check the number?" "Who?" asked a perplexed Coombs. "Your boss," the cashier retorted.[16]

The lesson is clear. Even though middle-class blacks are not likely to be refused service in restaurants and hotels as was James Weldon Johnson in the 1930s, like middle-class blacks described by Drake and Cayton in their study of blacks in Chicago during the 1940s, today's new black middle class continues to face the *uncertainty* of how they will be treated both in social settings and on the job. The struggle for access to public accommodations has been won; the struggle for respectability and humane treatment has not. Many middle-class whites resent sharing space and employment with blacks; others cannot shake the belief that blacks are only around to "fetchit" or, at least, that blacks cannot possibly have achieved notable success.

These lingering racist attitudes find expression in subtle as well as overt ways, subjecting blacks to embarrassment and humiliation. It is perhaps the many expressions of unconscious racism and persistent stereotypes of blacks that are most annoying since they have a way of causing "slips of the tongue" among whites who would never think of calling a black person "nigger." The possibility of encountering these inadvertent slips or conscious racist slurs are an ever-present reality to middle-class blacks and a source of strain that whites would have difficulty imagining. To avoid the possibility of public embarrassment or curious stares from whites, many of today's new black middle class either continue the practice of home entertainment or seek protection in numbers by only frequenting certain "black" restaurants or clubs. Another practice involves the racial wave syndrome, whereby blacks may frequent a popular restaurant's happy hour and are then replaced by whites later in the evening, or vice versa. The objectives are the same: security and comfort in numbers. When these blacks venture out into nontraditional recreational pursuits such as skiing or golf, they are likely to form *black* ski clubs, such as Washington's "Black Ski," or to participate in black fraternity-sponsored golf and tennis tournaments. While working side by side with whites in a wide variety of both upper- and lower-middle-class occupations today, relatively few members of the new black middle class are likely to socialize with their white colleagues outside of the work setting.

The work setting is itself the source of considerable anxiety and ambivalence both because of racial slurs, which one white general sales manager of a major bank in northern Virginia admitted "happens weekly in some business and social settings," and because of the feeling by many very capable black professionals that they are allowed to rise only so far in their companies or are treated unfairly in the distribution of merit pay in government agencies. One study of a federal government agency in Washington found that often those blacks with the best documentation of discrimination refused to press their cases for fear of reprisals. That these feelings of discrimination in employment are not simply the result of paranoia caused by past discrimination will be clear from a comparison of occupational and income data on middle-class blacks and whites presented in chapter 4.

# 4

# How Big a Piece?

## BLACK AND WHITE OCCUPATIONAL AND INCOME ACHIEVEMENTS COMPARED

A comparison of the old black middle class and new black middle class (chap. 2) revealed significant occupational gains, particularly among black males. No longer were middle-class black males to be found only in the traditional occupations of teacher, minister, lawyer, doctor, or entertainer. They could be found holding at least sixty-five different middle-class job titles by 1976. While real, however, these gains still left black males far behind whites, who held some ninety-seven job titles. Differences in the number of middle-class occupations was especially great at the highest level, the upper-middle-class stratum of professionals and managers, where white males were diversified into 68 percent more occupations than blacks. Although not so heavily concentrated in traditional occupations as in the past, five occupations still harbored black males disproportionately: social worker (3.3%), elementary (2.3%) and secondary (5.1%) schoolteacher, mail carrier (3.3%), and postal clerk (5.1%). In only two new occupations had they entered in large numbers—clerical supervisor (2.8%) and policeman (4.7%). By contrast, the only concentration above 2 percent found among white males was in the occupations of accountant (2.1%), secondary schoolteacher (3.3%), sales representative in retail (2.4%), and policeman (3.9%). In none did the proportion rise to 5 percent. In spite of impressive gains over the old black middle class, black males still lag far behind white males in the diversity of occupations to which they have found access.

It has also been noted that black males actually suffered a setback in the 1970s, experiencing a decline by 1976 in their share of jobs in the managerial and sales-clerical strata. There were increases at the professional level, but these were insufficient to offset their other losses, with the result that the actual proportion of middle-class black males *declined* between 1970 and 1976. While middle-class white males also suffered setbacks in the managerial and sales-clerical strata, the losses were compensated for by sharp gains at the professional level, so that their overall proportion in the labor force in 1976 was the same as it was in 1970. These patterns continued for the remainder of the decade, with the percentage of black males finally growing by less than one percent, ending up with 23.4 percent of all black male workers in the middle class by 1980 compared to 44.4 percent of all white males.

The experience of black females compared to white females was more favorable than that of black males in the 1970s, but only marginally. In part, this was because of sexist discrimination white as well as black females continue to experience in the labor market. Thus, both white and black females were still found to occupy a far narrower range of jobs than their male counterparts during the 1970s. Altogether, my 1976 survey found forty-five different white-collar occupations represented among black females employed full- and part-time and forty-eight among whites. A comparison of the occupations in which black and white females were most likely to be found makes it clear that white females have made more progress than blacks, even though more black females have worked full-time and have remained in the labor force for longer periods. Four of the six occupations in which black females were most frequently found were the traditional ones of registered nurse (9.9%), social worker (6.4%), elementary schoolteacher (14.6%), and secondary schoolteacher (2.3%). Two new occupations, retail sales clerk (5.3%) and secretary (8.8%), although traditionally female work, nevertheless represent gains for black women since they had been barred from these jobs before the passage of the Civil Rights Act. The nine most common occupations in which white females were found not only included five of those most frequently entered by blacks—registered nurse (6.4%), elementary schoolteacher (9.3%), secondary schoolteacher (5%), retail sales clerk (4.3%), and secretary (7.9%)—but also four in which black females were still scarce in 1976—recreation worker (2.1%), bank teller (2.9%), bookkeeper (6.4%), and typist (2.1%).

Unlike males, black females and white females continued to gain in all strata of the middle class during the 1970s, among professionals, managers, and proprietors as well as sales and clerical workers. This was true at middecade, when black males had lost ground overall and white males were able only to maintain their 1970 level. And it proved to be a trend that continued to the end of the decade. Black females had increased their representation in the middle class from 35 percent in 1970 to 49 percent by 1980. The proportion of white middle-class females went from 64 to 68 percent in the same period. Despite the impressive gains by black females, white females were still far ahead of blacks in the number of those who had made it into the middle class. More telling, all gains by white females during the 1970s were made at the upper-middle-class level; black females gained primarily in lower-middle-class jobs. Thus, clerical and sales jobs accounted for 72 percent of all new middle-class jobs gained by black women.

How can these meager occupational gains in the 1970s, especially by black males, be explained after the strong showing of the 1960s? When the size of the black middle class doubled during the 1960s, it appeared that equality of opportunity was finally becoming a reality at the middle-class level and that the days when an individual's race was more important than his or her diploma were coming to an end. Title VII of the Civil Rights Act had opened up jobs for which the old black middle class could not even compete. The 1970s revealed, however, that the crack in the door of opportunity which had opened during the previous decade was closed as soon as it was realized that keeping it open during times of economic stagnation meant head-on competition with blacks for the same jobs. When jobs were plentiful in the 1960s, blacks could be included without whites actually having to compete with them. When it became necessary to compete, blacks found themselves losing. What was thought to be a permanent change in the opportunity structure for blacks turned out to be a temporary lowering of barriers at a time of rapid growth in middle-class jobs. With a decline in the rate of growth of middle-class jobs in the 1970s, it became clear that opportunity had improved only slightly for blacks and that race was still very significant. In white businesses and even in government, the hiring of personnel is usually in the hands of whites, affording them the maximum capability to discriminate should they wish. Nor could blacks turn to black businesses for jobs. In 1977, the top 100 black businesses combined had only 8,389 employees.[1]

## WHO'S IN CHARGE?

It was pointed out earlier that once blacks have entered middle-class occupations, they often complain of discrimination in pay, promotion opportunities, or both. An examination of my 1976 data on supervisory status confirms that black males are far less likely to be supervisors than whites. For the class as a whole, only a little more than one-third (39%) of black males were supervisors, compared to more than one-half (56%) of white males. Only in the lower-middle-class stratum of clerical and sales workers did black males have the same proportion of supervisors as whites (28%). This, of course, is the stratum in which males have the lowest concentration and which—from a male standpoint—is the least desirable because of the lower salaries received compared to upper-middle-class jobs.

Unlike males, an almost identical proportion of black and white middle-class females in my sample were supervisors, a parity that held for all three strata. As will be seen, however, neither black female supervisors nor black male supervisors received pay equal to whites. While both black and white male supervisors were paid higher salaries than nonsupervisors, the white male supervisors' bonus was more than twice that of black male supervisors. The gap was not quite as great among black and white female supervisors, but white female supervisors were found to earn an average of approximately $1,200 more than blacks. Blacks were less likely to be promoted to supervisory positions, and if promoted, they gained less than whites from the move upward.

## Uncle Sam or IBM

The first breach in the solid wall of prejudice against the employment of blacks in middle-class jobs was achieved through employment in the federal government. Beginning with the postal service, which blacks managed to enter in the 1940s through civil service examinations, public service at the federal and state levels became the primary source of middle-class growth for a long time. In Washington, D.C., with its large bureaucracy, many blacks found middle-class employment as secretaries and midlevel professionals as well as in their traditional unskilled jobs. Thousands of blacks were successful in working their way up the GS ladder over the years, giving rise to one of the largest concentrations of middle-class blacks in the nation. The government, while traditionally providing a major opportunity for the development of the black middle class, has also been noted, however, for offering lower salaries than the private sector. With the enactment of the Civil Rights Act, pressure was brought to bear on private industry to include more blacks in their work force at all levels, thus potentially opening up new avenues to equality with middle-class whites.

Twelve years later, in 1976, black middle-class males were still far more likely than whites to find a job in government service than in the private sector. One-half of all black males in my 1976 sample, compared to only about one-fourth of whites, held government jobs. Furthermore, black males have not reaped the same income benefits as whites for taking jobs in private industry. While white middle-class males in the private sector earned an average of $2,000 more than those in government, black middle-class males in industry earned $2,000 *less* than those in government. White males earned more than blacks regardless of sector.

Black middle-class females were found to be even

more heavily concentrated in government than black males, having fully two-thirds employed there. By contrast, two-thirds of white middle-class females were employed in the private sector. While black as well as white females earned higher salaries in government than in the private sector, white females earned more than black females within government. The comparative earnings were about the same in private industry.

Government employment gave blacks their first real opportunity to pursue middle-class careers that went beyond serving the needs of the black community. But government employment has been a mixed blessing. In addition to the fact that government salaries are lower than those paid by private industry, attempts by the Reagan administration to cut expenditures by reducing the federal work force affected blacks disproportionately. In the early 1980s, when federal agencies were pressured to reduce the number of their employees, a congressional survey by the Federal Government Service Task Force found that minority employees in the federal government had been laid off at a rate 50 percent greater than nonminority employees. Particularly hard hit were middle and senior executives in grade levels 12 through 15, all members of the middle class.

## THE BOTTOM LINE: DOLLARS AND CENTS

In a very real sense, the bottom line of all comparisons of middle-class blacks and whites is income since, lacking other sources of wealth, the middle class is almost totally dependent on income for its standard of living. To understand whether or not middle-class blacks have caught up with whites, therefore, it is important to carefully compare their respective incomes. The discussion immediately following is devoted to comparisons of the incomes of *individual* males and females and to an exploration of the reasons for black-white income differences. In chapter 5, I turn to comparisons of family income and standards of living.

## THE BLACK MALE-WHITE MALE INCOME GAP: DISCRIMINATION OR HUMAN CAPITAL

The average income of all black middle-class males in my 1976 sample was $14,700. The average for white males was $19,300, almost $5,000 more. This finding was confirmed by national census data showing a similar income gap from 1976 through the rest of the decade. In the face of their recent occupational gains, how do we account for this large, persistent income gap? Is it simply an artifact of the different composition of the two groups in the sample, or is it a result of discrimination? We have already observed above that white middle-class males are more likely than blacks to be supervisors, to hold upper-middle-class jobs, and to work in the private sector—all characteristics associated with higher salaries. Could it be that the income gap—calculated for the entire group—is but a reflection of the presence in the samples of a larger number of white males than black males with these high income attributes?

One way to understand whether the income gap results from the different composition of the two groups or from discrimination is to determine whether blacks receive the *same payoff* as whites for the same income-producing characteristics. For example, we know that supervisors are paid higher salaries than nonsupervisors. But do blacks who are supervisors receive salaries similar to whites? If black supervisors receive *lower* salaries, then the income gap results not only from the higher number of white supervisors in the sample but also from the lower salaries of black supervisors.

Seven different factors known to be associated with income were examined in this analysis: level of education, type of occupation, supervisory status, sector of the economy, age, time on the job, and region. Through the use of the statistical technique of multiple regression, separate equations were calculated for blacks and whites to determine the return in dollars blacks and whites received for each of these seven characteristics.[2]

The results revealed that black males received lower returns than whites for *each* of the seven factors. For example, it was found that, with the same job, an additional year of education increased a white male's salary by $611 on the average but a black male's by only half as much, $306. Black males likewise did not receive the same return in income as whites for their occupational achievements. With upward mobility measured in terms of points on an occupational scale,[3] it was found that each point up the scale was worth an additional $93 in income to white males but only $72 to blacks. Further, when all other factors in the equation were taken into account, supervisory responsibility had no significant impact on the salaries of black males but added approximately $2,375 to the income of whites. We have already seen that the factor of sector works in opposite directions for blacks and whites. Whites gained by taking jobs in private industry; blacks improved their financial position by taking jobs in government. Whites, however, had more to gain by their choice, earning around $2,000 more on the average for employment in industry compared to blacks' $1,100 edge for working in government. Not surprisingly, blacks in the North and Midwest did better than those in the South, earning around $1,500 more on the average. Whites suffered no such handicap for choosing to live in the South.

We come, finally, to the effects of age and time on the job, indicators of work experience and seniority. One of the common complaints voiced by black professionals involves the benefits of seniority in terms of promotion and salary. The complaints are supported by this analysis. White males were found to receive more than four times as much added income as blacks for each additional year on the job, even though on the average blacks in the sample had slightly more seniority than whites. White males also profited more than blacks in their overall job experience, earning about three times as much as blacks for each additional year in chronological age. Translated into dollars and cents, this would mean that if we compared the salaries of a black electrical engineer and a white electrical engineer (occupational score 95) working for a private firm, both supervisors, aged 30, living in the North, and with the same amount of seniority, the black engineer would earn $15,625 compared to $20,608 by the white engineer, a gap of about $5,000 (fig. 8).

The example of the engineers points to serious discrimination in the manner income is allocated to middle-class males, but it does not tell us the amount of the overall income gap at the group level that is due to discrimination. Certainly, some of this gap results from differences in human capital, such as education, and from differences in occupational characteristics, such as supervisory status. But how much? This question can be answered with the aid of a standardization technique[4] controlling for differences in the composition of the two groups, while allowing the *process* or manner whereby income is allocated to blacks and whites to vary.

By substituting the characteristics of white males into the equation for black males, we get an estimate of the impact of the *less favorable composition* of black males on their income, such as fewer supervisors and lower occupational achievement. Solving for this equation revealed that the average income of black males would increase by only 8 percent, or about $1,094, if they had the same occupational characteristics as white males (fig. 9).[5]

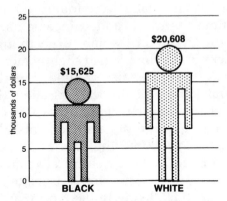

Fig. 8. The economic price of being black. Salary differences of black males and white males with the same characteristics in 1976: engineers, aged 30, supervisors, same seniority, working for private sector in the North.

However, when white males were given the group characteristics of black males without losing the advantage they hold in the income allocation process, on the average their income was reduced by 16 percent, or about $2,991—a change from $18,841 to $15,850 in 1976.

The greater reduction in average white male income when substituting black characteristics is a result of *differences in the process* of income attainment among blacks and whites. Given the way the system works for blacks, increases in income-producing characteristics such as education and seniority have relatively less impact on their income than they do among whites, because blacks receive considerably *lower rewards for the same characteristics*. While this means that white males with less favorable characteristics (than other whites) are more severely penalized than black males with less favorable characteristics (than other blacks), it also means that whites have more to gain from an improvement in those

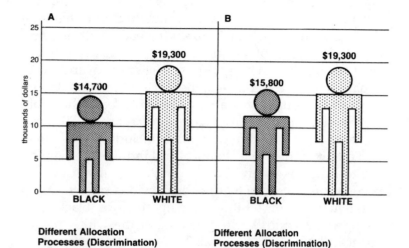

Fig. 9. Black and white male *group* salary averages. A = salary gap due to both discrimination and different characteristics, $4,600; B = salary gap due to discrimination alone, $3,500.

characteristics because of the higher income returns. For black males, it makes less difference if they earn an additional year of education or ascend the occupational ladder a few steps.

To earn an increase in income similar to that of whites, black males must have more education than whites, on the average, and be in higher occupations. These findings prove that the income gap between black males and white males is *primarily* a result of discrimination and supports the contention of black males that they must be "super niggers" (with higher credentials than whites) to receive the same occupational rewards as their white counterparts. What this means becomes clearer if we look more closely at the example of the black engineer and the white engineer with the $5,000 salary gap.

What would the income gap be if the black engineer had the advantage of age, say, ten years? Leaving the equation for the white male untouched but changing the age of the black male to 40 instead of 30, we find that the income of the black male is raised by about $680, to $16,305. The gap is still slightly over $4,000. What would the income gap be if the occupational score of the white male was about 15 points *lower* than that of the black male? An occupational score of 80 is assigned to several different jobs, including draftsman and credit man, while chemical and industrial engineering technicians receive scores of 79. By substituting an occupational score of 80 (for the previous score of 95) in the equation for whites, leaving that for blacks unchanged, we find that the income of the white male is reduced by $1,335, to $19,273. A gap of $3,648 still remains. Finally, if we substitute *both* the higher age and the lower occupational score in the equations for the black male and the white male, we find that the remaining income gap is still almost $3,000. In other words, a black middle-class male with the same education as a white male—both having supervisory responsibilities and working in the private sector but the black being ten years older and having an occupational score 15 points higher—still earns about $3,000 less than his white counterpart.

Such is the handicap, or "race effect," that black males face in the job market. Cumulatively, it means that black supervisors do not have access to the same type of supervisory positions as whites and are not rewarded as well; do not profit to the same extent as whites from work in private industry, work experience, seniority, and educational achievement; and suffer additional discrimination if they reside in the South. Income discrimination is therefore very much a fact of life among middle-class black males and one of the principal sources of economic inequality between the black and the white middle classes.

## THE BLACK FEMALE-WHITE FEMALE INCOME GAP: DOUBLE JEOPARDY, BLACK AND FEMALE

Black females experience the double discrimination of being black and female. With white females, they suffer from occupational restrictions and income inequalities in a male-dominated market. When compared with white females, it becomes apparent that they also suffer from the additional handicap of a process that rewards black females and white females differently—frequently to their disadvantage. This is not always apparent from a comparison of incomes, as the average incomes of black middle-class females and white middle-class females are similar. In fact, the average for black females in my 1976 sample was slightly higher than for whites, $9,843 compared to $9,721. The "average" black female in my sample, however, was slightly older than her white counterpart (39 compared to 38), had two years more seniority, and had worked more years since marriage. At the same time, her educational level was about the same as the white female's and her occupational score only slightly lower. A simple comparison of these characteristics would lead one to expect black females in the sample to exceed the average income of whites by far more than the $122 observed. Indeed, if black females had experienced the same income allocation process as whites, their average incomes would be about $1,700 higher, or $11,376 (fig. 10).

The incomes of black females and white females, though similar, thus result from very different processes. In general, for black females, income is a matter of having the *right educational credentials* and residence

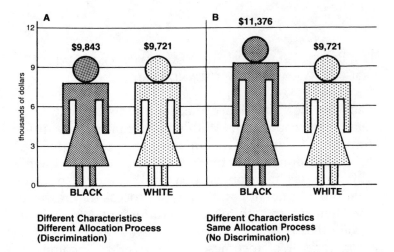

Fig. 10. Black and white female *group* salary averages in 1976.
A = different characteristics and different allocation processes;
B = different characteristics, same allocation process.

in the North, with lesser effects from occupational level
and seniority. For white women, it is a matter of the
sector in which they are employed and having supervisory responsibility, followed by the influence of seniority
and their labor market experience. These are striking
differences in the ways black middle-class females and
white middle-class females earn their incomes. Most
striking of all are differences in the income returns relative to education, supervisory status, sector, and region.

Neither supervisory status nor sector in which employed had a significant effect on the incomes of black
middle-class females *after* the effects of the other factors
had been taken into account. Yet these characteristics
were the most important for white females. In their
case, supervisors earned an average of over $3,000 more
than nonsupervisors, and those in government had
salaries almost $3,000 higher than those in private in-

dustry. And whereas black females in the North earned about $1,400 more than their counterparts in the South, white females earned similar salaries in both regions.

Each year of education was found to be worth about $720 in additional income to black females but had no statistically significant effect on the incomes of white females after the effects of the other factors had been taken into consideration. So important are educational credentials for the income achievement of black females that the point needs further comment. The fact that black females receive a *higher* return for education (after the other factors are taken into account) than white females does not mean that they are favored or have an advantage. It means just the opposite: on the average, with less education, white females can earn the same incomes as black females. This is the case because they are more likely to be hired and promoted to supervisory positions with less education than black females. For black females, education is essential. In fact, applying the standardization technique used for males reveals that *two-thirds* of the income of black middle-class females in the mid-1970s could be attributed to their education alone. If black females in the sample had received the same income return for education as white females, their average income would have been reduced to $2,260. While these are the most important differences in the ways black middle-class females and white middle-class females earn their incomes, there were a number of others that are worth noting.

Black females, for instance, gained far less income from seniority than white females, even though as a group they averaged two years more seniority. For each year on the same job, a white female could expect an average income increment of $185, compared to only $93 by black females. Similarly, white females profited more from labor market experience than black females in spite of the fact that black females had worked an average of eight years more than whites since marriage. In this case, labor market experience did not even have a significant effect on the incomes of black females once other factors—including seniority—had been taken into account, while white females earned an average of $30 more for each year of market experience over and above the $185 for each year of seniority. This is a meaningful difference, since one of the most commonly cited reasons for the lower incomes of females compared to males is their lesser market experience. This finding demonstrates that in addition to receiving a lower return for seniority, black females profit far less than whites from their years in the labor market.

Finally, type of occupation as measured by occupational score contributed significantly, though with moderate dollars, to the income of black females but had no statistically significant impact on white females' income after other factors were taken into consideration. This last finding increases the impression that black females, above all, must have the proper credentials if they are to earn substantial incomes, while white females are more likely to be highly rewarded for supervisory status, seniority, and overall labor market experience. Were black females to receive the same income return for supervisory responsibilities as whites but the same return they now receive on all other characteristics, their average income would rise by more than $2,000. Thus, if the process worked the same for black females as for whites, their average income would not only equal that of whites but would exceed it because of their greater job experience and seniority. The double jeopardy of being black and female takes a heavy toll. In the next three chapters, the analysis will move from the individual to the family level, comparing the living standards and life styles of middle-class blacks and whites.

# 5

# Life in the Middle: In Pursuit of the American Dream

In the mid-1970s, middle-class blacks felt an unprecedented optimism and confidence about their future. On the heels of a successful civil rights movement that had won legal access to whatever their money could buy, Title VII's new occupational promises, and an expanding economy, it seemed to most that their ship had finally come in. Not even the deep recession that shook the country from 1973 to 1975 seriously dampened this enthusiasm. By 1976, the country was recovering from what then appeared to be just another of the temporary setbacks that had recurred since World War II. The gas lines were gone and the future was rosy again.

## THE BEST OF TIMES?

The overwhelming majority of both black and white middle-class respondents in my 1976 survey voiced their optimism, saying that their lives were either "pretty satisfying" or "completely satisfying." Even clearer were the responses this national sample of middle-class blacks gave interviewers who showed them a stepladder with eleven rungs, numbered 0 to 10. Told to imag-

133

ine that the top rung represented the *best* life they could have and the bottom, the *worst*, 61 percent placed themselves in the middle (rungs 5–7) and only 13 percent on the bottom (rungs 0–4). Most striking of all were the differences in the assessments of their lives five years prior to 1976 and their expectations for life five years in the future. Almost one-half reported that they had experienced the worst possible life they could have in 1971, but only 4 percent held this expectation for 1981. *Two-thirds* looked forward enthusiastically to achieving what they believed would be the best possible life by 1981 (rungs 8–10). Needless to say, 1981 proved not to be the best of times, thanks to another recession, high interest rates, and high unemployment. But was the new black middle class accurate in its self-assessment even in 1976 when one-fourth placed themselves at the top of the ladder and another 61 percent in the middle? What had been the cumulative effect on their living standard of the gains of the previous ten years which were sparked by the civil rights movement and national prosperity? And how did the living standards of middle-class blacks and whites compare in the mid-1970s?

## ASSESSING THE LIVING STANDARD OF THE NEW BLACK MIDDLE CLASS

The best objective measure of overall living standard thus far developed comes from the Bureau of Labor Statistics (BLS). Beginning with the assumption that "maintenance of health and social well-being, the nurture of children, and participation in community activities are desirable and necessary social goals for all families" in our society, the bureau developed measures of the costs of maintaining an adequate standard of living.[1] In fact, budgets for three different standards of living were calculated, recognizing that an adequate standard can be achieved with different qualities and quantities of necessary goods and services. A family may provide its protein needs with chicken or sirloin steaks; clothing can be purchased at bargain stores such as Kmart or at high-priced, high-prestige clothing stores like Saks or Bloomingdale's. The resulting budgets reflective of possible consumer choices are termed the lower, moderate, and higher standards of living for an urban family of four.[2]

The lower budget corresponds to the bureau's earlier "modest but adequate" standard developed in 1959 and assumes that such families live in rental housing without air conditioning, perform many services for themselves, and use free recreation facilities in the community. The moderate and higher budgets are distinguished primarily by the quantity and qualities of goods and services consumed. Those at the higher standard have greater rates of home ownership, are more likely to pay for necessary services, have more complete inventories of household appliances and equipment, and in general consume goods and services of superior quality and quantity.

These three budgets correspond to our commonsense notions and experiences of differences in living standards. Most of us know families who, though not deprived or poor, are "just making it." Living in rental housing, they depend heavily on free community services, eat out only at McDonald's, and use television as a major form of recreation. Then there are those families that may or may not own their own home but who occasionally go to restaurants and concerts and can afford to shop at modest department stores. Finally, there are those whose homes we admire and who take vacations abroad, shop at prestige clothing stores, and in general are seen as quite comfortable. It is this last standard that most Americans are likely to associate with the middle class. This is the American Dream that most aspire to. While in the mid-1980s this dream has become somewhat tarnished by the inflated cost of housing and the higher cost of living in general, the three standards remain distinguishable and recognizable. Today, fewer middle-class families, black or white, are able to maintain this higher standard on one income, but in 1976—the point at which the new black middle class was consolidating and enjoying the gains of a decade—a single income was commonplace among whites. History may yet record the late 1960s and early 1970s as the "best of times," the end of the "Golden Age."[3] It is important, therefore, to examine the new black middle class's achievement during this period to see whether its optimism matched its objective living standard. Later, their living standard will be reassessed in the less heady times of the 1980s.

## MAKING IT—BUT ON TWO INCOMES

In fall 1976, the BLS budgets corresponding to the lower, moderate, and higher standards of living were $10,041, $16,236, and $23,759, respectively.[4] Using these figures, we can assess the living standards the new black middle class had reached by the mid-1970s and compare this achievement with that of the white middle class. Figure 11 reveals that middle-class black and white families both had average incomes close to the BLS higher standard. At $23,343, the average income of the white middle class was right at the standard while the average for blacks fell short by about $2,000. Since upper-middle-class blacks (professional-managerial) had an average income only about $500 less than the BLS higher budget, it is the greater percentage of blacks in the *lower* middle class (sales-clerical) that accounts for this $2,000 deficit for the class as a whole. About 39 percent of middle-class blacks in the sample were lower middle class,

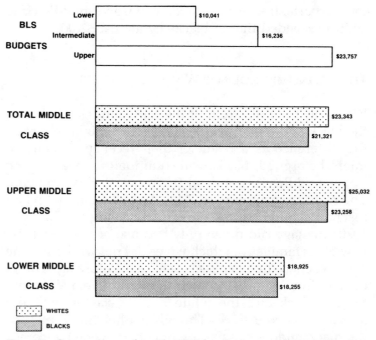

Fig. 11. Comparison of total 1976 family income of middle-class blacks and whites with Bureau of Labor Statistics budgets for 1976.

compared to 28 percent of whites. This higher concentration of blacks in the lower middle class is itself a measure of the gap remaining between the black and the white middle classes, especially given the much lower income of that stratum. At $18,255, the average income for lower-middle-class blacks was $5,500 *below* the requirement for a middle-class living standard. While lower-middle-class whites also fell short by $4,800, their percentage of the group was smaller than blacks. All in all, a significantly larger percentage of middle-class blacks than whites lacked the income to live up to the standard of their class as a whole. Nor had upper-middle-class blacks overtaken their white counterparts; the average income of upper-middle-class whites exceeded that of blacks by almost $2,000.

## THE ECONOMIC ROLE OF WIVES

Were this the full extent of the remaining gap between the black and white middle classes, we might minimize the difference as a result of their recency. In time, it might be argued, blacks will continue to move into the upper middle-class and, in the process, close the gap. The reality was otherwise. Most black families who had reached a middle-class standard of living by the mid-1970s managed to do so only because of two incomes. Few black families in which wives did not work full-time even reached the *intermediate* standard of living. This is evident from figure 12, which shows the average income for the black and the white middle classes with the *income of wives removed*. Though neither the white nor the black middle class as a whole had average incomes equal to the BLS higher budget, the gap between blacks and whites widened to around $5,000 when wives' income was removed. Without the income of wives, white middle-class families would *exceed* the BLS intermediate standard of living by several thousand dollars; black middle-class families would fall *below* the intermediate standard. Though both classes as a whole relied on the employment of wives to reach or approach a middle-class living standard, the need was far greater among blacks.

This need is even clearer from a comparison of husbands' incomes in families without working wives with husbands' incomes in families where wives worked full-time. The average income of all black middle-class males in families without employed wives was $16,200, or about $3,700 higher than that of husbands whose wives were employed full-time, but still below the inter-

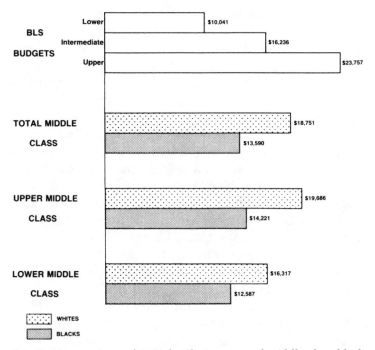

Fig. 12. Comparison of 1976 family incomes of middle-class blacks and whites, with income of wife removed, with Bureau of Labor Statistics budgets for 1976.

mediate budget. White husbands of nonworking wives earned $5,600 more than those whose wives worked full-time, having average incomes of $20,600 and $15,000, respectively. However, in only 24 percent of white families did wives work full-time, compared to 62 percent of black families. It was the relatively low incomes of some middle-class males, particularly black males, then, that made it necessary for their wives to seek employment.

This is confirmed by the responses of wives and husbands to questions about why wives worked. Seventy-three percent of black families and 53 percent of white families gave general "financial necessity" or the need to make some purchase as the reason. Only 20 percent of black wives cited personal considerations such as a career, need for independence, or a desire to keep active as their motive. Paralleling the higher incomes of white husbands, white middle-class wives were almost twice as likely to give personal reasons as their incentive.[5] While some wives among both blacks and whites worked in 1976, black middle-class families were three times as likely to depend on the incomes of both spouses to maintain or approach a middle-class standard. The lower incomes that black males received for the same amount of education, experience, occupation, and other income factors were translated into a lower standard of living for middle-class black families. It was a deficit only partially overcome by the full-time employment of 62 percent of black wives—another example of the continuing significance of race.

The high rate of wives' employment within the black middle class also had a negative impact on living standards. The BLS budgets assume that wives do not work. Thus, the additional costs of clothing, transportation, lunches, and, in some cases, child care associated with working wives are not represented. The budgets are therefore underestimates of actual costs when a wife works. Hence, many families are actually further from a middle-class standard of living than income alone indicates.

The economic role of wives was important to the black middle class in yet another way. More black than white families owed their middle-class position to the occupational achievement of the wife rather than of the husband. This was the case in one-fourth of black upper-middle-class families and more than one-third of the lower middle class. By comparison, only 7.3 percent of upper-middle-class white families and 16 percent of those in the lower middle class owed their class position to that of the wife. Concretely, this meant that there were black nurses whose husbands were carpenters, auto mechanics, and truck drivers as well as social workers and draftsmen. There were also black elementary schoolteachers with husbands who worked as construction laborers, painters, or carpenters as well as school administrators and teachers. While in some respects this may be a "neutral" fact without great consequences, economically it has a negative impact on the black middle-class living standard, since women with the same occupations as men earn lower salaries.

## HOW MUCH WEALTH?

Living standards, though assumed by the Bureau of Labor Statistics to be supported by income from salaries, are also affected by existing wealth and credit buying. How dependent was the black middle class in 1976 on plastic money, and what sources of wealth did they have to fall back on in case of need?

### *Savings*

The easiest form of wealth accumulation is through savings accounts. They can be added to in any increment, often through direct payroll deductions, and best of all, they remain available without penalty in case of need or financial emergencies. A savings account is the proverbial "nest egg" against a rainy day, hence its existence or nonexistence is itself an indicator of a family's economic well-being. Without a savings account, a family will have to borrow, do without, or make do with less in emergencies brought on by such common events as car repairs or a necessary trip, not to mention the satisfaction of such wants as a special purchase or a vacation.

Given the ease with which people can save, it is not surprising to discover that 87 percent of black and 93 percent of white middle-class families reported having a savings account or some kind of savings plan in 1976, with only minor variation between those in the upper- and lower-middle-class strata. Most also saved as frequently as monthly or every other month. Yet only 4 percent of middle-class blacks had accumulated savings of $10,000 or more, and only 19 percent had saved between $4,000 and $10,000. Over half had less than $2,000. By contrast, 17 percent of whites had $10,000 or more in savings, and only 40 percent had less than $2,000. These rates translated into an average of $2,800 in savings for middle-class black families and $4,200 for whites.

## Stocks

Stocks and bonds, the second most common form of wealth accumulation, are less flexible than savings accounts because of the requirement of outlays in fixed amounts and the risk of loss. In addition, there is the need for more knowledge, brokerage fees, the element of risk, and reduced access in case of emergencies. Ownership of stocks and bonds, therefore, is an indicator of greater economic security than are savings accounts. Here, again, we find whites far outstripping blacks. Middle-class whites were twice as likely as blacks to own stocks and bonds. Among those owning such wealth, whites were almost four times as likely as blacks to have accumulated values of $10,000 or more: 19 percent to 5 percent. Comparing only those families with stocks and bonds valued at $4,000 or more, we find the percentage of white owners is three times that of all blacks (fig. 13). Finally, over half of all black owners but less than 30 percent of whites reported total values of less than $1,000. Corresponding to the higher value of

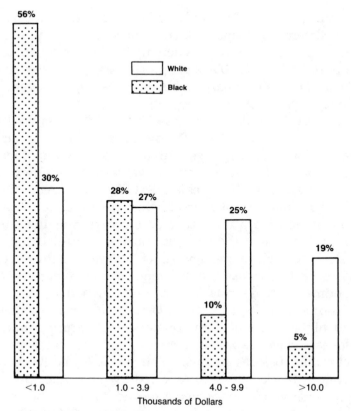

Fig. 13. Values of stocks and bonds owned by middle-class blacks and whites in 1976.

stocks owned by whites, average dividends received in the previous year (1975) were almost twice as high for whites ($645) than for blacks ($340). And both black and white upper-middle-class families earned between three and four times as much in dividends as those in the lower middle class.

*Property*

Property, including home ownership, is another form of wealth. While not a liquid asset, property appreciates in value, is part of a family's net worth, and can serve as collateral for loans to finance needed expenditures. Like education, home ownership has always had an important value for black people. As we saw earlier, the home served as an oasis in a hostile, segregated world. Hence, blacks made every effort to own their own home. By 1976, three-fourths of all middle-class blacks had managed to do so. Middle-class whites still surpassed blacks in this area, with 89 percent owning their own home. The average market value of homes owned by whites was also greater: $44,000 compared with $31,200. This was, of course, before the rapid appreciation of housing values that occurred during the late 1970s. Given that the price of housing appreciated at a faster rate in more prestigious neighborhoods, the effect has been to increase the difference in the market value of homes owned by blacks and homes owned by whites. It should also be noted that *lower*-middle-class whites had higher rates of home ownership than upper-middle-class blacks as well as homes of higher average market value. Besides homes, relatively few middle-class families, black or white, reported owning other property, and even fewer owned a second home. In the next chapter, we will take a look at ownership of cars and other goods that are part of an assessment of total living standard.

*Debts*

On the other side of financial wealth are existing debts that a family has incurred and a variety of expenses that must be met. Some of these, like insurance costs, are fixed; others, such as auto repairs and clothing, vary from month to month. Of interest here is a family's ability to meet these expenses out of existing income and the amount of disposable income remaining.

One major source of debts since the 1950s, when bank cards and other charge accounts began to proliferate, is credit buying. Seventy and 74 percent, respectively, of middle-class blacks and whites in my sample owned three or more credit cards. Only 11 percent of blacks and 6 percent of whites had none. (Since middle-class whites had more credit cards than blacks and upper-middle-class families of both races more than those in the lower middle class, the number of credit cards is itself a measure of financial standing or credit-ableness.) While having fewer credit cards and charge accounts, middle-class blacks depended more on credit buying than whites, a reflection of their lower incomes. Almost twice as many whites (31%) as blacks (18%) owed nothing on their accounts, and one-third of black families owed $1,000 or more compared to one-fifth of white families. Including those who owed nothing, this came to an average of $1,305 for all blacks and $980 for whites. Upper-middle-class black families owed most, on the average, but even lower-middle-class blacks had an average credit card debt exceeding that of upper-middle-class whites.

## Monthly Bills and Expenses

In 1976, these debts translated into monthly bills of $183 for blacks and $164 for whites, or about $354 and $317, respectively, in 1986 dollars. It should be noted that these debts exclude such regular expenses as mortgage, rent, and automobile notes. Corresponding to the higher value of the homes they owned, middle-class whites had higher mortgage payments than blacks, and those who rented had greater monthly rents. Far more whites than blacks also had cars fully paid for: 67 percent compared to 40 percent. A black middle-class emphasis on luxury consumption—particularly cars and clothing—is apparent here. In contrast to whites whose upper and lower middle classes had new cars in the same proportions, about 10 percent more upper- than lower-middle-class blacks had new cars. Correspondingly, fewer of them had cars fully paid for. Of all those in the middle class, upper-middle-class blacks also had the highest outstanding balance on cars and reported the highest average cost of repairs and maintenance (excluding accidents) for 1975.

The cult of clothes, criticized by Frazier in his 1957 book on the black middle class, *Black Bourgeoisie*, and noted by Drake and Cayton among middle-class blacks in Chicago during the 1940s and early 1960s, was still evident in the mid-1970s nationally. Both upper- and lower-middle-class blacks spent more on clothes, on the average, than their white counterparts. Upper-middle-class blacks, especially, spent considerably more than whites ($200 per month compared to $130) even though their families were smaller and incomes lower.

## Insurance Premiums and Health Care

While spending less per month for clothing and having lower car payments than blacks, middle-class whites spent more on health care and life insurance. This included slightly higher monthly premiums for both health insurance coverage and life insurance as well as higher out-of-pocket costs for health care not covered by insurance. Since it was the upper middle class of both races which had higher medical expenses not covered by insurance, medical costs after insurance reflect the quality and extent of medical care received rather than state of health. These out-of-pocket expenditures covered visits to a doctor for preventive care and minor ailments not covered by insurance as well as other costs remaining after insurance payments. Thus, it would appear that in general middle-class whites receive more adequate medical care than blacks and upper-middle-class families more care than those in the lower middle class.

Weekly expenditures for groceries did not differ significantly between blacks and whites or by strata within the middle class. Money spent on educational expenses for children was also approximately the same for black and for white families, on the average, though it was about twice as high in the upper- as in the lower-middle-class stratum. The advantage the middle class holds in terms of both a higher standard of living and the ability to transmit their position through education appears to be especially realized at the upper-middle-class level.

## OVERALL ECONOMIC POSITION OF BLACKS AND WHITES

In evaluating loan applications, banks will often request sufficient information to calculate an individual's net worth: the difference between existing assets and debts. We arrive at a measure of the total liability of a family—minus the amount owed on homes and other property—by adding the total amount owed on charge accounts and automobiles. Combining assets in stocks, bonds, and savings accounts yields a summary measure of liquid assets, or wealth—minus the accumulated equity in homes and other property. Information on the value of automobiles, the existing balance owed, and equity accumulated in homes (and other property) was not collected in this study. With these two exceptions, all other relevant data were gathered to calculate a family's net worth. How did the new black middle class compare to whites in the mid-1970s in total assets, debts, and net worth? How close to parity had they come?

The total outstanding *debts* of whites were only 62 percent of that owed by blacks, or an average of $1,725 compared to $2,774 (the equivalent of $3,336 and $5,365, respectively, in 1986 dollars). The gap was greatest at the upper-middle-class level, with blacks having an average liability of $2,900 compared to whites' $1,770. But the white middle class, with an average of $6,900 in total assets, had almost two and one-half times the wealth of middle-class blacks. In the upper middle class, white wealth exceeded that of blacks by *more* than two and one-half times. Translated into a measure of net worth, this reveals a tremendous gap in the overall economic position of middle-class blacks and whites. The average net worth of middle-class whites in 1976 was 250 times that of blacks, or $5,518 compared to $22. Among whites, it is those in the upper middle class who had the largest average net worth: $6,700 compared to $2,500 for those in the lower middle class. In contrast, upper-middle-class blacks actually had a *negative* net worth (–$12) as measured above, while that of the lower black middle class was less than $100.

Of course, these are averages, that is, many whites as well as blacks have larger net worths than these figures, and many also have smaller net worths. It should be remembered, too, that equity in homes and automobiles is not included in these calculations. Were they included, middle-class blacks would no doubt have a larger net worth. At the same time, the higher rate of white home ownership as well as the higher market values of whites' homes would show an even larger gap in net worth. The negative net worth of upper-middle-class blacks (without the inclusion of home equity) reflects their struggle to maintain an upper-middle-class living standard with fewer financial resources than whites. Recall that to maintain an income equal to the BLS higher budget required two full-time earners in black upper-middle-class families while upper middle-class whites *exceeded* that budget by $2,000, in most cases with one earner. The new black middle class, in spite of significant progress, was still far short of economic parity with whites in the mid-1970s.

A family's net financial worth, while important, may have an impact on living standard only infrequently or only at a particular stage of life, such as when children reach college age, in times of extended illness, or when a special purchase is desired. To assess the economic condition of the black middle class on a month-to-month basis (a more natural unit), additional summary measures were constructed based on monthly debts and expenditures. The first measure included only fixed monthly debts such as payments on credit accounts, mortgage or rent, and health and life insurance premiums. The second represented expenditures for groceries, medical bills, clothing, automobile repairs, and transportation. Adding the two measures produced a third measure of total monthly expenditures, or living costs. Fixed monthly expenditures were calculated separately from variable expenses to provide a better understanding of racial differences in expenditure patterns.

## DIFFERENCES IN BLACK AND WHITE EXPENDITURES

It has been seen that the white middle class spent somewhat more than blacks for mortgages and rent as well as for life and health insurance premiums. This was interpreted as positive for whites in that these costs represent higher levels of consumption, that is, goods and services of superior quantity and quality. Differences in monthly bills for charge accounts were not great, with blacks paying a slightly higher average amount. When combined into the composite measure, we find, not unexpectedly, that it is middle-class whites who pay slightly more in fixed monthly debts.

The average monthly costs of groceries, car repairs, and gas for transportation did not differ significantly between blacks and whites. Medical expenses not covered by insurance were higher for whites while blacks spent more on clothing—a trade-off between health and style. The overall average cost of expenses in this category is slightly higher for blacks than for whites. The emphasis on appearance, demonstrated by excessive amounts spent on clothing and cars, reflects the status anxiety of new arrivals to the middle class, who are overeager to convey the impression of having arrived. It is a familiar pattern noted by Thorstein Veblen among newly arrived upper-class whites in the early part of this century.[6] In the case of middle-class blacks (old and new), there is the additional element of feelings of marginality in a racist society that will not accept them for their achievements alone. In this environment, the *visible* trappings of the middle class serve to assuage personal status and racial anxiety, establish distance from the black masses, and announce to whites that they are just as good.

When the above two measures of fixed and variable costs are combined, racial differences in expenditures balance out, resulting in almost identical average monthly expenses for blacks and whites. Not to be forgotten, however, are the *different consumption patterns* of blacks and whites and the conclusion that whites maintain a higher standard of living in the areas of housing, life insurance, and medical care. Overall, also, upper-middle-class families of both races spent more monthly than those in the lower middle class, reflecting their ability to maintain higher living standards.

## Living Well But Spending It All

The costs of goods and services by themselves do not fully reveal or exhaust the meaning of economic condition. Even if two families are able to purchase the same things, one may do so only by spending all or most of its earned income while the other may have a considerable amount remaining. Thus, one family will find itself able to accumulate savings for emergencies, but the other will not. To determine the amount of disposable income remaining after the payment of bills, two additional indexes were developed. One calculates disposable income by subtracting total monthly expenses from monthly income after taxes; the other subtracts expenses from the income of husbands alone.

The latter index gives an indication of what disposable income would be if only the husband worked. Subtracting total expenses from husbands' incomes before taxes left middle-class black families with an average monthly income of only $136, compared to $417 for whites. It is to be remembered that these figures represent the economic condition of middle-class families *without* the financial contribution of wives. Not surprisingly, black families can barely meet their essential expenses when wives do not work. In fact, 38 percent of black families and 21 percent of white families would not be able to meet all their monthly expenses under these circumstances. The need for wives to work is even greater than these figures suggest since income taxes were not subtracted from husbands' income, nor had the costs of education and recreation been calculated.

This helps us understand the responses of families with working wives to the hypothetical question of what would be the impact of the wife's loss of her job. Asked whether this would cause a real financial crisis, just make things difficult, not be much of a problem, or not be a problem at all, almost *two-thirds* of both black and white families with working wives said that the loss would either make things difficult or cause a real crisis. Of these, 22 percent of blacks and 19 percent of whites fell into the "real crisis" category. While the racial differences in these responses are not great, it should be recalled that in 1976 two-thirds of middle-class black wives worked full-time compared to only one-fourth of middle-class white wives.

Since a large number of wives work, particularly among blacks, what is the effect of their contribution in terms of providing the family with a greater amount of disposable income? With black middle-class wives' income included, the average monthly family income remaining after taxes (calculated at 20% in 1975) once all expenses were paid was $420 and $270, respectively, for upper- and lower-middle-class black families. Among whites, average disposable income was $446 in the upper-middle-class stratum, $200 in the lower.

If educational expenses and the costs of recreation, vacations, personal care items, and home repairs were included, disposable income would be even less and in many cases would disappear altogether. Reflecting this fact, one-third of all black middle-class families said that their income was inadequate. In the lower-middle-class stratum, the number of those who felt this way rose to 40 percent. This inadequacy was expressed by only one-fourth of lower-middle-class whites and even fewer in the upper middle class. Almost half of all middle-class blacks also responded that meeting monthly bills was either a little difficult or very difficult. Recreation and vacations were areas most frequently mentioned as presenting difficulties by both blacks and whites who felt their incomes to be inadequate. When funds are limited, these expenses seem to be the first to drop from the budget. All in all, most black middle-class families required two incomes to meet usual monthly expenses and maintain a middle-class living standard. Even with two incomes, most of those in the lower middle class are not able to meet that goal, and neither stratum has much remaining for wealth accumulation.

Most upper-middle-class whites are able to maintain

a middle-class living standard without the need for wives to work, and many have sufficient surplus to accumulate savings. Lower-middle-class white families without two incomes are a bit better off than lower-middle-class blacks with two incomes but still are unable to maintain a middle-class living standard. As a group, however, they comprise a smaller proportion of the middle class than lower-middle-class blacks.

## In Time of Emergencies

With so many middle-class black families having to spend all or most of their earnings for daily living expenses, how did they handle unexpected financial needs? Families were asked both how they believed they would handle an unexpected expense of about $500 or more and how they had managed an actual major expense during the preceding twelve months. In response to the former, hypothetical question, the majority of blacks (63%) and whites (69%) felt they would be able to use money from their savings. What was unexpected was the relatively large percentage who anticipated having to turn to bank loans, finance companies, relatives, or friends for such a small amount: 37 percent of blacks and 30 percent of whites. That these responses do indeed reflect actual economic state is confirmed by differences in the responses of those in the upper- and those in the lower-middle-class stratum. Almost two-thirds of upper-middle-class families expected to cover an unexpected expense of $500 from savings, compared to only 49 and 58 percent of lower-middle-class blacks and whites, respectively.

About one-fourth of both blacks and whites had experienced an actual expense during the previous twelve months. What kind of financial emergencies were these? And how were they actually covered? For almost one-half of these middle-class blacks (42%), the expense involved house or car repairs; for another 32 percent, it was a medical cost. The opposite was true of whites. Only among upper-middle-class whites, however, were these expenses met from current income or savings by over one-half (55%) of the group. The majority of blacks and lower-middle-class whites had taken out a loan, sacrificed something, or borrowed from a friend or a relative. The reason for the discrepancy in the way respondents expected to pay for a hypothetical expense and the actual way in which a real expense was met is unclear. The number who actually had such an expense was small (only 25%) and may not have been representative of the entire sample. It is also possible that the actual expenses were greater than $500.

A number of other questions were asked in an attempt to discover in what areas middle-class families might have unmet needs. These touched on car repairs and medical and dental care during the previous two months, expenditures that are often unmet or delayed for considerable periods when finances are tight. However, less than one-fifth of middle-class blacks or whites had been unable to take care of needed car repairs and even fewer—about 10 percent—reported having to postpone needed medical or dental care.

## THE ACID TEST: SURVIVING WITHOUT A JOB

One of the benefits of life in the middle class is economic security. Having a good, steady job is one aspect of this security; a nest egg in the bank is another. We have already seen that in most cases, the nest egg that most middle-class blacks had been able to accumulate was rather insubstantial. Just how insubstantial becomes even more striking if we calculate its worth in terms of the length of time it would enable a family to survive with neither the husband nor the wife employed. It is true that few middle-class workers ever face involuntary unemployment; yet the knowledge that all bills and everyday expenses can be met for some time should the unthinkable occur does provide an added sense of security. After all, the severe recession of 1973–1975 and the recurrent recessions the United States experienced into the early 1980s demonstrated that postwar levels of prosperity and growth have begun to taper off, leading into uncertain economic times. Just how long could middle-class black families maintain the standard of living reached by 1976 without either spouse working?

By dividing a family's total assets (savings and stocks) by its monthly income after taxes, we obtain a figure representing the number of months during which it could continue its current living standard while unemployed. Using this standard revealed that the new black middle class that had emerged by the mid-1970s could continue its living standard for only *two months* without anyone in the family working. The average middle-class white family had resources to survive at the same level for more than twice as long: 4.3 months. As noted earlier, averages do not reveal the whole story, since considerable variation both above and below the mean exists. Almost one in three (31%) black middle-class families actually had assets totaling *less than one month's* take-home pay, compared to one in six (17%) white families.

A more conservative means of estimating the black middle class's ability to survive during unemployment is its ability to keep the bill collectors away. Using this standard, we find that black families could pay their fixed bills (mortgage or rent, credit accounts, and insurance premiums) for just over half a year (7.5 months) and white families, a little over one year (13.7 months). When we add total monthly expenses (including food, clothing, transportation, car repairs, and medical care), the ability to survive without work is reduced to less than three months (2.8) for blacks and about half a year for whites (6.6 months). Both upper-middle-class blacks and whites had the resources to pay bills for a *longer* period than families in the lower-middle-class stratum of their respective groups, though the superiority of upper-middle-class economic resources is far greater among whites. In fact, lower-middle-class whites had sufficient savings to pay total bills for slightly longer (3.9 months) than upper-middle-class blacks (3.4 months).

These calculations underlie the reality of the Marxian tendency to place white-collar employees in the ranks of the working class along with blue-collar workers. Almost all have in common the need to work continuously for someone else to maintain their respective living standards. The difference between white-collar and blue-collar workers, as pointed out by Weber, is the greater educational skills of those in the white-collar sector, skills that enable them to obtain higher salaries, more fringe benefits, and stabler employment conditions than blue-collar workers. Nevertheless, this should not obscure the fact that none of those in the middle class are independently wealthy. For most, and especially for middle-class blacks, the level of wealth accumulation is not sufficient to allow survival for even half a year without unemployment compensation and borrowing.

## WAS BLACK MIDDLE-CLASS OPTIMISM JUSTIFIED?

The question raised at the beginning of this chapter, was the optimism of the new black middle class in 1976 well founded? has to be answered negatively. While many upper-middle-class blacks had managed to reach a middle-class living standard, this was true of few in the lower middle class, the stratum that made up the bulk of the new black middle class. Nor had the new black middle class been as successful as whites in accumulating any wealth in the form of savings, stocks, bonds, or property. While total expenditures of blacks and whites were similar, whites consumed more basic goods and services such as housing, life insurance, and health care, and blacks spent more on consolidating their newfound position by acquiring clothes and cars. Black middle-class families ended up with higher debts and less disposable income after expenses.

Even that level reached by the mid-1970s was dependent on the full-time employment of the majority of black middle-class wives. Without the economic contribution of wives, most black families would not have come close to a middle-class standard of living, and few could have survived at their present standard for more than a few months without employment.

The optimism of the mid-1970s, then, grew out of the *relative* gains blacks had experienced during the previous ten years in access to restaurants, hotels, theaters, lunch counters, and other community facilities as well as in greater access to jobs and the resulting rise in real income. There is no doubt that the civil rights movement and a booming economy had improved life for all blacks and especially for the new black middle class. At the same time, comparisons with middle-class whites have shown that these gains had left the new black middle class well behind the living standard achieved by whites. In chapter 6, I will continue the comparison with a look at a wide range of goods and services consumed.

# 6

# Consumption: Where, What, and How Much

A middle-class living standard is reflected in wealth and income. It is also visible in the consumption that results. In calculating three standards of living, the Bureau of Labor Statistics differentiated urban standards by the quantity and quality of goods consumed. Those at the higher budget level, the middle class, were distinguished from those at the intermediate level primarily by greater home ownership, possession of more household appliances and equipment, and generally consuming goods and services of superior quality and quantity. Some of the quality difference is blurred today by the availability of name-brand items through sales and discount houses. Still, we can certainly expect overall class distinctions in the amount of goods and services consumed. To assess living standards of middle-class blacks and whites more completely, I collected information on a great variety of material possessions. I also asked about shopping habits, since type of store is a rough indicator of quality of goods bought.

## OF CASTLES AND CARRIAGES

In fairy tales, princes always lived in castles, and Cinderella was instantaneously transformed from rags to riches by her ride to the ball in a magnificent carriage.

158

The house and the "ride" today remain two of the most visible signs of living standard. The two-story brick house with a Mercedes in the driveway is all most people need to label the next-door neighbors upper middle class. As we saw earlier, most middle-class families (75% of blacks and 89% of whites) owned their own homes, although, on the average, the homes of whites had a higher market value. Also, whites owned somewhat larger homes than blacks. Among home owners and renters taken together, whites still lived in larger homes than blacks—an average of 6.6 rooms compared to 6.3. With an average of 6.8 rooms, upper-middle-class whites maintained the largest homes, followed by upper-middle-class blacks whose average was 6.5. Despite the emphasis placed on home ownership, middle-class blacks still lagged behind whites in quantity and quality of this most important item.

What about the 25 percent of blacks and 11 percent of whites who were renters? Was this by choice or by economic necessity? When asked if they would like to buy a home, 64 percent of black renters and 55 percent of white renters replied that they would. Of these, the majority felt they would succeed in this ambition. Of those who did not expect to buy, the primary explanation given was economic. About two-thirds of home owners also thought they would be able to buy a home at the time of the survey if they did not already own one. Far more blacks in the upper middle class (69%) than the lower middle class (53%), however, thought they could buy in the mid-1970s, while whites in both strata were about equally confident of their ability to do so (67% and 61%). Again, most home owners who said they could not buy a house if they did not already own one gave a financial reason of some sort, for example, not having enough money, monthly payments being too high, or houses being too expensive.

Advertisements frequently characterize automobiles

as the biggest investment a family is likely to make after a home. Automobiles also signify freedom and prestige for their owners. The typical picture of a split-level suburban home includes a two-car garage. Blacks, in particular, are often seen as placing emphasis on the prestige afforded by a large, expensive car. Thus, there are two aspects to be considered: the car as a utilitarian object contributing to the overall living standard of a family and the car as a sign of prestige. Considering the variety of models on the market, information was not collected on the type of car owned or on cost. Respondents in the survey were asked to indicate the number of cars owned and the age of first and second cars. These two pieces of information provide additional insight into living standard, with age of cars serving as a very rough measure of prestige value.

Not surprisingly, relatively few members of the middle class owned no car, although the rate was almost twice as high for blacks (9%) as for whites (5%). The popular image of middle-class families as "two-car families" was only partially borne out: only a slight majority of black families (54%) and 60 percent of white families owned two or more cars. When ownership patterns are broken down by stratum, it becomes apparent that the two-car family image is far truer of upper- than of lower-middle-class families. Within the black middle class, 60 and 46 percent, respectively, of upper- and lower-middle-class families own two or more cars; among whites, 63 and 54 percent. In evaluating these similarities, it should be noted that given the much higher rate of employment among black wives, black families have a far greater need for two cars.

What were the ages of first and second cars? Here, again, popular images are shattered. Comparing first or only cars, we find that less than one-third of both blacks and whites owned new cars (1–2 years old). Almost one-half owned cars that were three or four years old, and the rest drove even older cars. The biggest difference was in the age of cars owned by upper- and lower-middle-class blacks. About 10 percent more in the black upper middle class owned new cars, and 10 percent more of lower-middle-class black families had cars that were five or more years old. Among whites, no variation by stratum was found in age of car. Since a higher percentage of upper-middle-class black families owned new cars than upper-middle-class whites (35% compared to 29%) as well as lower-middle-class blacks, it seems that the image of driving high-priced prestige cars fit a small segment of upper-middle-class blacks but not middle-class blacks as a total group. On the whole, second cars were much older than first cars, with about two-thirds of blacks (62%) and whites (68%) owning second cars that were five or more years old.

A car, although admittedly one of the most important purchases a family makes, represents only a small fraction of a family's total consumption. To determine the overall standard of living of middle-class blacks, information was collected on the ownership of about fifty-five different items. Unfortunately, it was not possible to determine the quality and age of each item; nor was it possible to learn whether items were purchased or received as gifts. Assuming these contingencies to be distributed randomly among both blacks and whites, however, the resulting comparisons should yield an accurate picture of the material possessions of the black and white middle classes. Respondents were also queried about their shopping habits for additional clues about living standard, especially quality of goods bought.

## WHERE

Were members of the middle class to be found only in the best stores, or did they also look for sales and shop at discount stores? It was found that over two-thirds of all middle-class families—black and white—regularly looked for sales. At the same time, only 12 percent of all middle-class blacks and 16 percent of whites shopped regularly at discount stores such as Kmart and Zayre. Perhaps the key to understanding this seemingly contradictory behavior is that all stores, even the most expensive, have sales that make it possible to purchase both quality and prestige items at lower costs. Discount stores, for many, often represent goods of inferior quality and prestige. What, then, did those who "sometimes" shopped at discount stores—slightly over half—buy there? Middle-class blacks most frequently purchased household items (88%), school supplies (74%), personal care products (66%), and, somewhat less frequently, garden and lawn care products (59%), clothing (40%), and sporting goods (37%). Whites most frequently bought household goods (82%), garden and lawn items (72%), school supplies (66%), personal care products (65%), and, sometimes, sporting goods (48%) and clothing (37%). Products about which there is most likely to be concern over quality and prestige—sporting goods and clothing—were the least frequently bought at discount stores.

Clothing expenditures, unlike many of the other items mentioned, may involve a substantial part of the family budget. Having great image value, clothing is bought as much for achieving prestige and a particular image as for utilitarian purposes, hence the popularity of brand names and prestige stores such as Saks Fifth Avenue and Bloomingdale's. To find out where middle-class blacks bought clothing for themselves and their children, they were asked if they *usually* shopped at the more expensive stores such as Saks or its equivalent, at less expensive but good clothing stores, at good department stores, at discount stores, wherever they could find a good buy, or through catalogs. We have already seen that middle-class blacks spent considerably more on clothes than whites—even though they had lower incomes and smaller families. This was taken to be evidence of the continuing emphasis on clothes that Drake and Cayton and Frazier noted in the forties, fifties, and sixties. Was this also manifested in the kind of stores in which they shopped?

Apparently not. Only 8 percent of blacks and 6 percent of whites shopped *regularly* at expensive clothing stores for themselves, and even fewer shopped there for their children. Only about one-fifth of both blacks and whites even habitually frequented "good clothing stores." About one-half of black families and white families indicated that they usually shopped for clothing at department stores. From another perspective, however, it can be said that about 28 percent of middle-class blacks and 27 percent of middle-class whites went to either expensive or good clothing stores. Given the lower income of blacks, it was expected that proportionally fewer blacks than whites would shop regularly at such stores. But, in fact, they could be found shopping at the best clothing stores in the same proportions as whites. Since the majority of these prestige-conscious black shoppers came from the upper middle class, we can conclude that it is a *small group* of *upper-middle-class* blacks and a few in the lower middle class who perpetuate the "conspicuous consumption" pattern of the past. The majority are either shopping at department stores or wherever they can find good prices. It is primarily through this small group of middle-class blacks who shopped at prestige stores, together with the overall higher expenditure by most middle-class blacks for clothing, that the cult of clothes continued into the 1970s.

## WHAT AND HOW MUCH

What material possessions and how much of them had the black middle class managed to accumulate by the mid-1970s? The answer can be found in a review of their inventories in the five areas surveyed: durable household goods, small electrical appliances, home entertainment items, sporting goods, and power tools. Cumulatively, these items give us a glimpse into the middle-class home during this period.

## HOUSEHOLD GOODS

Household items were divided into three categories: durable goods, furnishings, and small appliances—altogether, twenty-two different products. Those in the first category include many of the essential labor-saving devices characteristic of the modern home, such as washing machines and driers, vacuum cleaners, air conditioners, and, more questionably essential, home freezers, dishwashers, and sewing machines. Families were not asked about such truly essential items as stoves and refrigerators. The list of durable goods included central air conditioning and window air conditioning units in addition to those mentioned above.

The most common household item, after the stove and refrigerator, was the vacuum cleaner, which was owned by over 90 percent of both blacks and whites. Next came the washing machine, found in 82 percent and 92 percent of black and white homes, respectively. Far fewer blacks (69%) had a clothes drier, and approximately three-fourths owned a sewing machine. Central air conditioning was found in less than one-third of the homes of both blacks and whites, probably because this feature usually was not built into older homes. Slightly over one-half of both blacks and whites, however, had window air conditioning units. Ownership of dishwashers, a necessity to some and a luxury to others, presented the biggest racial differences in this list of household goods: twice as many middle-class whites

(60%) as blacks (30%) owned this convenience. Home freezers, another nonessential appliance, were owned by only about 40 percent of both black and white middle-class families. It should be emphasized, however, that in six of these eight appliances, the rate of white ownership exceeded that of blacks by from 6 to 30 percent. Upper-middle-class households also consistently exhibited higher rates of ownership than the lower middle class, especially among whites. Reflecting the racial differences in possessions, the index of ownership of durable goods (established by adding the number of items owned) was 4.6 for middle-class blacks and 5.4 for middle-class whites.

The racial gap was smaller in the case of household furnishings. Over 90 percent of blacks and whites owned bedroom and living room sets. Dining room sets were found in the homes of 84 percent of blacks and 75 percent of whites. Most homes also had wall-to-wall carpeting. In addition, about half had room-size rugs. Where multiple ownership was possible, such as in the case of wall-to-wall carpeting and bedroom sets, whites generally owned more of each item than blacks. The index of ownership for these five household furnishings was the same for middle-class blacks and whites: 3.9.

The nine small electrical appliances surveyed were toasters, mixers, blenders, electric can openers, coffee makers, electric knives, electric food warmers, electric toothbrushes, and garbage disposals. The first five were common household items, that is, they were found in the vast majority of black and white middle-class homes. In this category, toasters were the most common, owned by over 90 percent of blacks and whites; electric can openers, the least common, were found in 77 percent of all homes.

There was a large jump in ownership rates for the remaining items. Forty-seven percent of middle-class blacks and 59 percent of whites owned an electric knife, but less than 20 percent of blacks had the remaining three products—electric food warmers, electric toothbrushes, and garbage disposals. By comparison, these items were owned by between 25 and 33 percent of white families. It had been thought that garbage disposals—a very convenient and relatively inexpensive appliance—would be found in far more middle-class homes. But this was not the case. Higher rates of ownership by white families were again reflected in the ownership index for small electrical appliances: 5.8 for whites and 5.1 for blacks.

Among both blacks and whites, these appliances were also found far more frequently in upper-middle-class than in lower-middle-class homes. For instance, 81 percent of upper-middle-class black families owned blenders, compared to 72 percent of those in the lower middle class. Among whites, 91 and 83 percent, respectively, in the upper- and lower-middle-class strata had blenders. These interstrata differences were reflected in ownership indexes for small appliances: 5.4 and 4.7 for upper- and lower-middle-class blacks, and 5.9 and 5.6 for upper- and lower-middle-class whites. Note that in the case of these appliances, lower-middle-class whites have a higher ownership index than upper-middle-class blacks. The *overall* ownership index combining durable goods, household furnishings, and small electrical appliances was 13.6 for all middle-class blacks and 15.1 for all middle-class whites.

There were two categories of home entertainment items in the list of material goods. One category, consisting of seven items, covered photography paraphernalia: 35mm cameras, instamatic cameras, movie cameras, slide projectors, movie projectors, movie screens, and enlargers. The other category was made up of ten items: color television sets, black-and-white television sets, complete stereo systems, component stereo systems, tape recorders, radios, cassette recorders, portable bars, built-in bars, and pool tables. These products obviously vary considerably in cost and frequency of use. Enlargers and pool tables are not only expensive but involve special interests that many may not have even if they can afford them. Instamatic cameras, television sets, radios, and stereo systems might be called general interest entertainment items and are probably owned much more widely.

Among the photography equipment, only instamatic cameras were owned by most families: 69 percent of all blacks and 77 percent of all whites. Approximately one-fourth of black families and between 37 and 45 percent of whites had movie cameras and screens and 35mm cameras. Even fewer owned either slide projectors or movie projectors, and only 5 and 6 percent, respectively, of blacks and whites owned enlargers. Ownership indexes were correspondingly low: 1.8 for blacks and 2.7 for whites.

In the second category of home entertainment items, radios, television sets, and stereos led the list in terms of rates of ownership. Over 80 percent of middle-class blacks and whites owned at least one color television set, and most owned a black-and-white set as well. Almost every family in the sample, black and white, also owned one or more radios. Complete stereo systems were owned by over half of all blacks (65%) and whites (54%), while about 10 percent fewer families owned the more expensive separate component systems. In fact, separate component systems, cassette recorders, and tape recorders were all found in approximately half of all homes. The other three products in the list, pool tables, built-in bars, and portable bars, were owned by relatively few families, less than 20 percent of both blacks and whites.

One of the most interesting findings about this group of home entertainment products is that, along with the set of home furnishings discussed above, it is the only group in which blacks have higher rates of ownership of some items: black-and-white television sets, both types of stereo systems, tape recorders, pool tables, and both types of bars. This no doubt reflects the fact that black people have always placed great emphasis on home ownership and traditionally have centered much of their social life in the home. The practice, necessary during the period of segregation when most recreational and social establishments in the community were closed to blacks, seems to have become part of the black culture. By the mid-1970s, however, recreational and social establishments had been legally open to blacks for about a decade. In the discussion of life style (chap. 7), we will see to what extent this new access to the community changed the recreational life of the new black middle class. It should be remembered that, open accommodations laws notwithstanding, many of these establishments either still found ways to bar the participation of blacks or made them uncomfortable when present. Differences between blacks and whites in ownership rates across the two sets of home entertainment products balance out to some degree, so that ownership indexes combining them are not very different: 7.1 for blacks and 7.5 for whites. Lower-middle-class blacks have the smallest combined index, 6.3, followed by lower-middle-class whites, with 7.0. Upper-middle-class whites have the highest combined index, 7.7; upper-middle-class blacks, 7.6.

Of the many sports possible, families were asked about eight different products involving seven sports: bowling, golf, tennis, skiing, bicycling, boating, and camping. These sports vary tremendously in terms of skill required, time expenditure, and cost. There are also different cultural traditions involved. Golf had not yet caught on among blacks by the mid-1970s, though the success of Arthur Ashe in tennis had raised the participation rate in that sport. Should a Lee Elder or

Jim Thorpe reach the degree of fame in golf long held by Arthur Ashe in tennis, perhaps the pattern might change. In this period, however, only 11 percent of middle-class blacks owned golf clubs, compared to 42 percent of whites. Perhaps because of the expense involved, about three times the percentage of upper-middle-class blacks (16%) relative to those in the lower middle class (5%) owned golf clubs. Tennis had reached a much higher level of popularity among middle-class blacks, with 40 percent owning rackets—25 percent less than whites. Here, too, there was a sharp difference found between the upper and the lower middle class, with upper-middle-class blacks twice as likely to play tennis as lower-middle-class blacks. These interstrata differences also existed among whites but were not as great. Even fewer blacks owned skis than golf clubs. Although the percentage of whites owning skis was also low (15%), it was still five times the rate of blacks.

The most common outdoor recreational item found in middle-class homes was the bicycle, which was owned by 62 percent of blacks and 76 percent of whites. One-fourth and one-third of blacks and whites, respectively, also owned bowling balls and shoes. The least common items were boats and campers. Only 2 and 4 percent of middle-class blacks owned a boat or camper and only 13 and 10 percent of whites. Ownership indexes for sporting goods were 1.7 for blacks and 2.9 for whites.

The final category of goods in the inventory consisted of four types of power tools: power lawn mowers, electric drills, electric saws, and electric sanders. With such a high percentage of home owners, it was expected that most families would at least have power lawn mowers. However, only slightly more than half of all black families owned one. But for whites, the number was 77 percent, a gap far greater than that in home ownership. Two-thirds of whites also owned electric drills, compared to less than one-half of black families. Electric saws and sanders were even less common, although in both cases, more whites than blacks had them. Indexes for tool ownership for blacks and whites were 1.5 and 2.5, respectively.

## HEALTH CARE AND LIFE INSURANCE

Beyond material possessions, the areas of health care and life insurance must be considered. The amount and quality of the medical care received is certainly one of the most important aspects of a family's living standard. And life insurance—depending on type—can serve both as a kind of wealth accumulation and as protection in the event of death.

### Health Care

Regardless of class, there is a strong association between good health and health care, particularly preventive health care. Preventive health care, however, often entails a visit to a doctor for a routine checkup or a visit early in an illness when the cost is not likely to be covered by insurance. We have already seen that the cost of medical and dental care not covered by insurance was somewhat higher for whites than for blacks. This was interpreted as being a result of whites' more frequent use of medical and dental care. The relationship of health care to standard of living is also apparent in the higher percentage of lower-middle-class blacks and whites who had postponed needed medical care compared to those in the upper middle class.

To determine the extent to which middle-class blacks received preventive medical care, families in the survey were asked about the frequency of both medical and

dental checkups for various members of the family in
the previous year (1975). It was found that significantly
more blacks than whites had had *no* dental checkup
during this period. Looking at husbands and wives
separately, we find that 38 percent of black husbands
and 27 percent of white husbands did not visit a dentist
for an entire year, while 31 and 16 percent, respectively,
of black wives and white wives failed to do so. The
percentage of those not visiting a dentist rose to a high
of 42 percent among black lower-middle-class husbands. At the other extreme, substantially more white
husbands and wives had two or more dental checkups
within the year.

Differences in dental checkups between black and
white middle-class children were even more extreme
than found in their parents, with 26 percent of black
children but only 10 percent of white children having
gone without a checkup in the previous year. Correspondingly, almost one-half of white children, compared to slightly more than one-fourth of black children,
had two or more checkups. These statistics point to a
surprisingly low rate of preventive dental care within
the black middle class, especially among lower-middle-
class families. The situation was more encouraging in
the area of health care. In two-thirds of all black families,
both husband and wife had a physical checkup the
previous year, compared to one-half of whites. And in
only 16 percent of black families and 18 percent of white
families had neither spouse received an annual physical.

## Life Insurance

Information was collected on both the extent of life
insurance coverage and the amount. It was found that
in the majority of families, at least one spouse was
covered by some type of life insurance. Most frequently,

both spouses and children were covered or just husband and wife. Only 9 percent of black families and 4 percent of white families had no life insurance coverage for any member. Other racial differences in insurance coverage were not great.

Blacks and whites did differ rather strikingly in the value of policies held by husbands. For the class as a whole, the *average* value of policies held by white husbands was twice that of blacks: $39,000 compared to $20,000. The policies of black lower-middle-class husbands were the smallest of all, averaging only $13,000. At an average of $44,000, upper-middle-class white males had the best coverage. But even lower-middle-class white husbands had more coverage, on the average, than upper-middle-class black husbands: $30,000 compared to $24,000. Differences in the insurance policies held by wives was minimal, averaging $12,000 for blacks and $11,000 for whites. Although life insurance coverage was extensive among both blacks and whites, therefore, white families had much greater protection in the event of the husband's death.

## THE LIVING STANDARD OF THE NEW
## BLACK MIDDLE CLASS: A FINAL ASSESSMENT

What does this analysis of material possessions, life insurance, and health care tell us about the living standard of the new black middle class? It should be recalled that in developing its three budgets, the Bureau of Labor Statistics did not provide a *list* of goods against which we can compare each level. Except in the case of food consumption, where nutritional standards have been scientifically established, the BLS standards were set by a survey of the *actual choices* consumers made at each budget level, using the intermediate budget as the norm of an *adequate* standard of living. Those families living *above* the adequate level, whose consumption of goods and services go beyond the strictly adequate, were viewed as living at a higher standard. It is this higher standard of consumption that I have taken as the middle-class standard.

This approach coincides with the general notion of the middle class as those who have gone beyond the point of "just making it" into the area of "the good life." Here consumption is not based merely on need; it spills over into areas of convenience and even luxury. To distinguish this higher standard, BLS merely speaks of the consumption of *greater quantities* and *higher quality* goods and services—relying on consumer choices to determine exactly *how much* and *what quality*. For instance, in the sixties, home ownership was placed at 85 percent for the higher budget level, compared to 75 percent for the intermediate level. Likewise, the norm of health care at the higher standard, what I am calling middle class, included a major medical insurance policy in addition to the basic hospital-surgical insurance coverage found at the other two levels.

Following the BLS approach, I have taken the *actual consumption of middle-class whites as the norm in assessing the living standard of the new black middle class.* In other words, the findings tell us: "This was the living standard of middle-class whites in the mid-1970s." And, "This is where middle-class blacks stood by comparison." These results are a benchmark against which future comparisons can be measured.

The overall most important, most consistent finding throughout this comparison has been that middle-class whites consumed more goods and services than blacks. With few exceptions, this was true as we moved from home ownership through household products, recreational items, sporting goods, and power tools to health care and life insurance. In the case of home ownership, for instance, 75 percent of black middle-class families owned their own home, 10 percent below the BLS norm for the middle class and 14 percent below the 89 percent level of middle-class whites. White middle-class homes, on the average, were also larger and had higher market values. Single and multiple car ownership was also slightly higher among whites even though, with the majority of black wives working full-time, black families had a greater need for two cars.

Middle-class blacks, however, spent more on clothes as a group and a proportion equal to whites shopped regularly at expensive, prestige, or good clothing stores. This was seen as a continuation of the conspicuous consumption patterns of the old black middle class—but on a very limited scale. The majority of middle-class families—black and white—regularly looked for sales and over half shopped at least sometimes at discount stores.

Comparisons of the indexes of ownership reveal higher rates of white ownership of material goods than blacks in all but a few cases: dining room sets and some home entertainment products. In most other cases, middle-class whites owned more—often substantially more—household and recreational products than blacks. In some instances, especially in that of small electrical appliances, even lower-middle-class whites owned a greater variety of products than upper-middle-class blacks.

In the area of health care, it was found that middle-class whites were more likely to visit a doctor for minor ailments and had more frequent dental checkups, though more blacks had had a complete physical the previous year. Life insurance coverage of white husbands substantially exceeded that of blacks, and even lower-middle-class white husbands carried more life insurance than upper-middle-class black husbands.

The second most important finding in this analysis of middle-class living standards is the gap between the upper- and lower-middle-class strata. Among both blacks and whites, upper-middle-class families were found to enjoy a substantially higher standard of living than those in the lower middle class. This was apparent from a comparison of the average family incomes of the two strata, amount of wealth possessed by each, and their ability to survive without a job. It was also reflected in lower-middle-class ownership of a far more restricted list of household and recreational products, less life insurance coverage, and lower levels of health care. Overall, upper-middle-class whites enjoyed the highest living standard. They were followed by upper-middle-class blacks, although in some areas, lower-middle-class whites were better off. The least well-off were lower-middle-class blacks.

Finally, it is important to remember that, whether in the upper or lower middle class, most black families needed *two* full-time incomes to reach even the standard of living revealed in this analysis. That is, by the mid-1970s, even with two incomes middle-class blacks as a group had not reached the living standard attained by whites with primarily one income. Whether looking at income, wealth, ability to survive without a job, or the consumption of goods and services, it is clear that the new black middle class had not overtaken whites of the same strata ten years after the civil rights movement and national prosperity combined to bring it into existence.

# 7

# Life Style: And the Living Is Easy, or Is It?

Chapter 1 called attention to the distinction between classes and status groups. *Class* is a direct outcome of an individual's position in a society's economy through the control of capital or through an occupation. *Status* is subjective, emerging from the community's evaluation and ranking of its members. Class and status yield distinct stratification systems in a society. The first is associated with *life chances*, the ability to consume needed goods and services such as shelter, food, and health care. The second is related to *life style*, which goes beyond needs into the area of subjective preferences and tastes. While distinct, the two stratification systems are correlated. The wealthiest families are generally in both the upper class and the highest status group, the poorest at the bottom of both. Assembly line workers do not normally associate with engineers off the job or belong to the same clubs. Bankers are not usually found in bowling alleys.

This correlation of class and status has not been true historically among blacks. As we saw, the highest status group, the elite, contained individuals from different classes. Even today, the two highest black status groups come from the middle class rather than the upper class because blacks do not yet have a capitalist upper class. It is the highest of the two status groups that I have called an elite. It is this group, also, that Frazier charged imitated the life style of the white upper class or upper-middle class and that was criticized for its "conspicuous consumption." Some scholars have argued that Frazier's criticism was never true or at best was true of only a small percentage of middle-class blacks;[1] others have argued that middle-class blacks no longer engage in conspicuous consumption but instead have adopted a life style in keeping with their true class position.[2]

It should be reemphasized that life style concerns *status positions* of middle-class blacks, not class position. The distinction is not always easy to make. For instance, the Bureau of Labor Statistics assumes that most middle-class families own a late model car. From the standpoint of life chances, the significance of a car is purely utilitarian—it provides reliable transportation. The particular *model* chosen goes beyond the question of life chances into life style. Presumably, a compact Ford or Datsun will serve the same function as a Mercedes or Cadillac. But the Mercedes and Cadillac connote luxury and high status. In general, when we go beyond matters of practicality, such as size, safety, and durability, in purchasing products, we are moving from considerations of life chance to life style. Beyond type of material goods, life style touches on values, use of leisure time, organizational affiliations, and neighborhood. What kind of life style did the new black middle class pursue in the mid-1970s? Understanding this requires a look at the above facets of life style in relation to this group.

## CASTLES AND GHETTOS

In the discussion of the black middle class's living standard, it became clear that a single generalization cannot be made about the new black middle class as a whole. Significant differences existed not only between blacks and whites but also between upper- and lower-middle-class blacks. Particularly with respect to clothes and automobiles it was found that a small percentage of mostly upper-middle-class blacks were more likely to have new cars and shop regularly in high-status clothing stores. These choices that go beyond living standards to those of life style set the stage for the present chapter. What kind of differences were there in the life styles of middle-class blacks and whites in the mid-1970s? And what were the variations between blacks of the upper and lower stratum? In what kinds of neighborhoods do they live?

Part of the American dream is to own one's own home, in a safe neighborhood and compatible with one's perceived status. Thus, a move up the economic class ladder frequently is accompanied by efforts to physically move out of old and into new housing and neighborhoods. In this process, personal taste influences needs, mingling status and class considerations. Neighborhoods differ significantly in quality of housing, schools, recreational facilities for children, racial mix, convenience, and attractiveness, and those individuals and families who move up the class ladder have the greatest opportunity to choose neighborhoods with the optimal combination of desirable qualities—whatever these may be.

While prestigious neighborhoods exist in all parts of a metropolitan area, for whites newly arrived in the middle class, the search for a better neighborhood increasingly came to mean a move to the suburbs. This trend accelerated after the Second World War, and by 1960, the suburban population had exceeded that of central cities for the first time in U.S. history. Though it has been demonstrated that the suburbs are by no means the homogeneous domain of the middle class they were once thought to be, it is also clear that among whites, suburbanization has been and continues to be a movement led and numerically dominated by the middle class.[3] This does not mean that the white middle class has deserted the central city. Cities continued to have exclusive neighborhoods where the rich and wealthier upper-middle-class families were to be found. One has only to think of the East Side of New York and Georgetown in Washington, D.C. Many young white upper-middle-class couples have also been moving back into the city, often rehabilitating old structures and at times completely displacing longtime black residents and changing the character of whole neighborhoods. In Washington, D.C., where this pattern was more accelerated than in most other cities with large black populations, prestigious Capitol Hill went from predominantly black to predominantly white in just a few decades, while other areas continue to be transformed by this invasion.

Thus, the white middle class moves freely about the entire metropolitan area in search of more desirable neighborhoods. What is not clear is the extent to which blacks have been able to improve their neighborhood location as they moved into the middle class, much as white ethnic groups from Europe have done.[4] Involved in this question is the problem of residential segregation and the degree to which the black middle class has been able to free itself from this constraint in seeking better neighborhoods.

TO THE SUBURBS—GINGERLY

Researchers of black suburbanization in recent years are unanimous in agreeing that the movement of blacks into the suburbs has not approached even remotely that among whites in terms of volume or composition.[5]

While the black population grew faster than the white population in the suburbs during the sixties, the total number of suburban blacks remained small. Blacks constitute 12 percent of the population, yet in the twelve largest SMSAs in 1970, blacks made up only 6 percent of the total population of the rings.[6] Among these twelve, the black proportion in suburbs ranged from a low of 1.6 percent in Boston to 9.1 percent in Washington, D.C. In only six out of the fifteen largest urbanized areas in 1970 did the number of suburban blacks exceed 25,000.[7] Nationally, blacks constituted only 4.9 percent of the suburban population in 1970.

Following the recession in the early seventies, the pace of black suburbanization increased in the nation as a whole and in the fourteen largest metropolitan areas where blacks were particularly concentrated.[8] By 1980, their percentage of the suburban population had risen to 6.1. While this represented faster growth than in the sixties, the number of suburban blacks remained far below their proportion in the nation. Much—though not all—of this movement continued to be spillover into suburban areas adjacent to black urban neighborhoods. The exceptions were the increasing numbers of upper-middle-class blacks choosing predominantly white neighborhoods.[9] This new pattern was too recent, however, to change the overall distribution of suburban blacks. They remained concentrated in the less affluent and predominantly black neighborhoods. Black suburbanization in the seventies was also very uneven, with Washington, D.C., and Los Angeles accounting for 21 percent of the total national increase in black suburbanites during this decade.[10] As blacks moved in greater numbers into the near suburbs, also, many whites were moving farther out into the fringe counties, sometimes called exurbia.

A large part of the blame for the slow pace of black suburban growth, as many researchers have observed, falls on racial barriers erected by whites to prevent similar choices by blacks.[11] Unlike generations of white ethnics who immigrated to the United States from Europe, blacks have not found these barriers of discrimination and residential segregation lowering as they moved up the economic ladder. Most black migrants to the suburbs, including those in the middle class, have had to settle in expanding black enclaves or areas from which whites were fleeing.[12] In some cases, these areas were merely extensions of central city ghettos or suburban developments built exclusively for blacks. Others were old industrial towns whites were leaving for newer developments. The primary factor behind this residential segregation in the suburbs has been racial discrimination. As Karl Taeuber observed, "The evidence . . . shows that the suburbanization to date has occurred with the same racially discriminatory channeling of black residents into selected localities that characterizes central cities."[13]

## NEIGHBORHOODS

Thwarted in their efforts to improve neighborhood surroundings by a move to the suburbs, middle-class blacks have long attempted to carve out enclaves for themselves. But with what success? There is evidence enough of solid black middle-class neighborhoods, such as Pill Hill in Chicago, Southwest Atlanta, Striver's Row in New York City, the Gold Coast in Washington, D.C., and Palmer Woods in Detroit, to indicate that middle-class blacks, no less than whites, have attempted to form exclusive neighborhoods. These "leading black neighborhoods," as *Black Enterprise* called them,[14] reflect the constraints of racial residential segregation in their composition. Fifty-five percent of some forty such neighborhoods identified by *Black Enterprise* in 1974 had black populations ranging from 70 to 100 percent. The combined population (black and white) of these communities was only 716,459, an indication that we must look elsewhere for the neighborhoods where most members of the new black middle class live.

To gain a better understanding of the character of neighborhoods in which most middle-class blacks lived, additional data were collected on the characteristics of the census tract from which the black and white middle-class samples for this study were drawn. Census tracts approximate neighborhoods in size, and since the Census Bureau publishes considerable data on their characteristics, they are convenient units to use in such comparisons as this. In addition, an index was used to compare the degree of class and race segregation existing in black and white middle-class neighborhoods. The latter will be discussed first.

The particular segregation index used takes into account differences in the size of the subpopulations of a given unit, such as racial groups or classes.[15] I interpret this index here as the probability of whites living in middle-class black neighborhoods or of blacks living in middle-class white neighborhoods. Alternately, when examining the degree of class segregation, this index reports the probability that middle-class blacks will meet skilled or unskilled working-class residents in their neighborhoods. The values of the index can vary from zero to 100 percent. The *lower* the index, the *less likely* is one group to encounter the other in their neighborhood. Indexes were calculated for each SMSA and summarized for an entire region.

As noted above, a number of recent studies have found that residential segregation in the sixties and seventies decreased very little or not at all from levels of the previous decades.[16] Since these were studies of the entire black and white populations, regardless of class, it may be that changes in the level of residential segregation among the middle classes went undetected. Data from the present study revealed that this was not the case. In the neighborhoods in which the majority of middle-class blacks lived, the average probability that whites would live there too was 20 percent in all three regions. In some areas, the probability was as low as 8 or 9 percent, and in Palm Beach, Florida, it was only 4 percent. In only two metropolitan areas was the probability of blacks meeting whites in their neighborhoods as high as 40 percent.

White middle-class neighborhoods were even more segregated than those of the black middle class. The average probability of blacks living in white neighborhoods was 4 percent in the South, 2 percent in the Northeast, and 1 percent in the north central region. In only one case, Birmingham, with a probability of 18 percent, was the chance of whites meeting black residents in their neighborhoods greater than 6 percent.[17] The higher degree of residential segregation in white middle-class neighborhoods reflects differences in black and white residential patterns. While most metropolitan blacks live in the central cities, almost twice as many whites in these areas live in the suburbs as in the central city. The higher degree of segregation in white middle-class neighborhoods reflects the small number of blacks who have found their way to the suburban middle-class areas favored by whites.

In their search for desirable neighborhoods, middle-class families have generally attempted to carve out enclaves containing only members of their own class. This results, in part, from the cost of housing in such neighborhoods but also from deliberate attempts to develop unique life styles apart from other classes. To what extent have middle-class blacks as well as whites attempted to segregate themselves residentially from other classes, and to what extent have they succeeded? Existence of some exclusive upper-middle-class neigh-

borhoods is evidence enough of the desire of middle-
class blacks to live in prestigious surroundings. Analysis
of census tract data for middle-class blacks and whites,
however, demonstrated that middle-class blacks have
been far less successful than whites in carving out such
exclusive neighborhoods. Neither middle-class blacks
nor whites as a group lived in neighborhoods completely segregated from the working class, but data from
the 1970s show that the black middle class lives in much
closer proximity to other classes.

In the Northeast, the *average* percentage of middle-
class blacks in any neighborhood was only 38 percent,
compared to 62 percent for whites. Other residents in
neighborhoods where the black middle-class lived were
about as likely to be from the unskilled as the skilled
working class. In white middle-class neighborhoods,
they were far more likely to be members of the skilled
working class. White middle-class neighborhoods were
only slightly less segregated in the north central region.
Black middle-class neighborhoods hardly existed at all
there, since in those neighborhoods where the majority
of middle-class blacks lived, there were slightly more
skilled working-class than middle-class black residents
and only a slightly lower proportion from the unskilled
working class. In the South, the white middle class had
been most successful in carving out niches for themselves, the black middle class the least successful. The
likelihood of whites having skilled or unskilled working-
class neighbors in the South was only 20 and 11 percent,
respectively. The likelihood of blacks having unskilled
working-class neighbors was 39 percent, higher than
the probability of their having skilled working-class
neighbors (30%) or even middle-class neighbors (31%).

Of course, neighborhood mixtures vary from SMSA
to SMSA within regions for both blacks and whites.
Only in Washington, D.C., however, did the proportion
of the black middle class in neighborhoods where the

majority lived reach 50 percent. Just the opposite was true for whites. In only one SMSA, Cleveland, was the proportion of the white middle class within these neighborhoods less than 50 percent. Given these findings, there are grounds to question the very notion of black middle-class neighborhoods except for small residential pockets such as those described in *Black Enterprise*. While few members of the black middle class live in inner city ghettos, the vast majority share neighborhoods with large numbers of both skilled and unskilled working-class blacks. The idea of a black middle class living in social isolation from the other classes is largely a myth. As the data show, it is only the white middle class that has succeeded in controlling its environment to a large degree.

## Neighborhood Quality

Differences in the race and class composition of black and white middle-class neighborhoods are reflected in socioeconomic indicators such as income, education, and quality of housing. Median incomes of white middle-class neighborhoods are uniformly higher than those of black middle-class areas. In about half the white middle-class neighborhoods, median family incomes in 1970 ranged between $10,000 and $15,000, the equivalent of between $28,000 and $42,000 in 1986. In the majority of black middle-class neighborhoods, the median fell below $10,000, the equivalent of below $28,000 in 1986 dollars.

Black middle-class neighborhoods also had substantially larger numbers of households with incomes below the poverty level and fared poorly on other indexes of socioeconomic well-being. Relatively few individuals in black middle-class neighborhoods had any college education in 1970, and even fewer had completed four or more years of college. As might be expected from the lower incomes, the value of homes was lower in black neighborhoods and the homes there were smaller. It is not surprising, then, that of those who said that their incomes were inadequate, 44 percent of blacks, compared to 23 percent of whites, felt their incomes were inadequate for the housing they desired. Middle-class blacks were also far less satisfied with their neighborhood environments than whites, with only 23 percent of blacks compared to 44 percent of whites feeling very satisfied.

## Social Life: Out of the Cave at Last

Living in a segregated world, the old black middle class pursued a social life behind the closed doors of their homes or of black social clubs—a practice that earned them the nickname "cave dwellers." Frazier also criticized them for their frivolous life style, especially their frequent card games, lavish home entertainment, cotillions, and dances. Drake and Cayton, in their study of blacks in Chicago, documented the accuracy of such charges up to the early sixties.[18] As the new black middle class emerged in the late sixties and early seventies, with most of its members rising from the humble origins of working-class families, what happened to the insular and pretentious life style of the black middle class? Did they take advantage of their hard-won access to the recreational facilities of the larger community, or did they, too, remain homebound?

To find answers to these questions, black middle-class families were asked in 1976 about their social life and the frequency of home entertainment and recreation outside the home. Their answers revealed considerable change from the patterns found among the old middle class. No longer did the home appear to be the center of middle-class social life. Almost half of all middle-class blacks had not entertained in their homes during the month prior to the survey. This was true of only one-fifth of whites. Somewhat more lower-middle-class black families (52%) than upper (40%) had *not* entertained, but in both strata whites were far more likely to have entertained at home and to have done so more frequently. Almost twice the percentage of middle-class whites as blacks had entertained in their homes two or more times during the previous month. Even a higher percentage of *lower*-middle-class white families (48%) than upper-middle-class blacks (41%) had entertained that frequently.

If that one month can be taken as typical of the life style of middle-class blacks in the mid-1970s, then there was no longer any sign of the weekly round of home socializing characteristic of the past. Middle-class blacks were far more likely to seek entertainment outside the home, going out an average of 3.6 times per month, compared to about 4 times per month by whites. Within both races, upper-middle-class couples went out somewhat more frequently than those in the lower middle class. Nor did middle-class blacks spend lavishly on either home or community entertainment; the average for both forms for the previous month had been $122 for blacks and $134 for whites.

What type of entertainment did middle-class blacks seek outside their homes? To find this out, families were asked to list up to six different activities they engaged in *regularly* each month. Since only about one-third of all couples mentioned more than two activities regularly engaged in monthly, only the first two activities given will be examined.

Leading the list were dining out, movies, and sporting events. These were the most frequent recreational activities engaged in by 61 percent of all middle-class blacks. Only 10 percent said they regularly participated in more social recreational activities such as parties, card games, socials, clubs, and visiting friends. Another 8 percent placed church activities as their regular recreational outing. Clearly, most middle-class blacks had moved from the home to the community in search of recreation by the mid-1970s. Dining out was the most frequently chosen outing for almost 30 percent of upper-middle-class blacks, more than twice the proportion of those in the lower middle class.

Since more whites of the upper (45%) than the lower (31%) middle class chose dining out as the most frequent recreational event, we can see the effect of income on life style. Lower-middle-class blacks were more likely to participate in less costly activities such as movies, sporting events, or home socials. The three activities most frequently engaged in by blacks—dining out, movies, and sporting events—were also first on the list of whites, except that sporting events were a more frequent activity than movies, particularly for the upper middle class.

Plays and other cultural activities were very low on the list for both blacks and whites, being the choice of only 5 and 6 percent of blacks and whites, respectively. By the mid-1970s, the "tube" had also begun to fill many of the leisure hours of middle-class blacks and whites, with one-half of blacks and two-fifths of whites reporting that they spent three or more hours daily watching their favorite programs. Another third of both groups watched two hours per day. In spite of the heavy dose of television, more than two-thirds of middle-class blacks and whites also found time to keep up with current events by reading the newspaper daily.

## VACATIONS

In the "old days," middle-class blacks found themselves hampered in their movement around the country, no less than in their own communities. Driving through the South usually meant a packed-chicken-dinner, non-stop trip, as there was not the opportunity to stay at motels or eat in restaurants along the way. Even when traveling through the North, blacks could not be sure how they would be received at a hotel or restaurant. By the mid-1970s, this had all changed legally. What was the impact of open accommodation on the vacationing habits of middle-class blacks? How often did they take vacations, and what were their destinations? The information collected with respect to these questions revealed the influence of class as well as race.

Upper-middle-class families among both blacks and whites were far more likely to take an annual vacation than those in the lower middle class and to have two or more weeks paid vacation rather than just one. Almost 70 percent of upper-middle-class black and white families said they took a vacation yearly, but only 49 and 55 percent of lower-middle-class blacks and whites did so. Most upper-middle-class black (74%) and white (80%) families had *actually* taken a vacation during the previous year, about 10 percent more than the lower middle class of each race.

From their answers to questions about their destinations, it was clear that the new black middle class was moving about more freely than its predecessor. Only one-fifth made the homes of relatives the usual destination for their annual vacation; most either went to recreational sites somewhere in the country or did both. The principal difference in the vacation destinations of blacks and whites was the smaller percentage of whites who visited only relatives for their annual vacation and the larger percentage who went primarily to recreational sites. Upper-middle-class blacks were also less likely than those in the lower middle class to only visit relatives. Two-thirds of all blacks who did *not* take an annual vacation cited financial reasons, compared to only

40 percent of whites. Whites were more likely to give lack of time or another reason not related to finances for not vacationing every year. The amount spent on vacations reflected these differences in financial ability. On their most recent vacation, the average spent by all blacks was $600; the average spent by whites, $700.

By the mid-1970s, middle-class blacks were also taking vacations abroad. Forty percent had done so by 1976, most during the previous five years. And, of these 40 percent, almost half had vacationed outside the United States two or more times. By contrast, 50 percent of middle-class whites had taken a vacation abroad, 43 percent two or more times. Those who had never traveled outside the United States for a vacation, particularly blacks and lower-middle-class families, were most likely to cite financial reasons. The financial consideration is also apparent from the larger percentage of upper- than lower-middle-class blacks who had gone abroad for a vacation. It can also be seen from the average amount spent on such vacations, $1,000 by blacks and $1,200 by whites ($1,934 and $2,321 in 1986 dollars), almost twice the amount spent on a vacation in the United States.

Destinations were influenced by both preference and cost. About half of all blacks who went abroad had visited one of the black Caribbean or Bahamian islands on their last vacation, while another 28 percent went to Canada. The cost factor is seen in the larger percentage of lower-middle-class blacks who went to Canada rather than the islands or Europe. Middle-class whites, particularly those in the upper middle class, visited Europe, the islands, and Canada in almost equal numbers.

A NEW TYPE OF JOINER

The old black middle class confined its organizational life primarily to social clubs and fraternities. Drake and

Cayton found relatively few blacks involved in organizations devoted to self-help or political goals. Most female joiners, according to one woman in a self-help club, fell into the "butterfly group," that is, those interested only in frivolous pastimes such as bridge playing and teas. While male social clubs provided a forum for political discussions, they too were primarily devoted to socializing.[19]

What impact did the racial and political activism of the sixties have on the organizational life of the emerging new black middle class, many of whose members had been involved in the movement or benefited directly from its results? To find an answer to this question, members of the new black middle class were asked about the organizations they belonged to and about their civil rights and political activities. Of those who belonged to any organization (about one-half), only 14 percent held membership in organizations devoted to socializing, such as fraternal, athletic, or hobby groups. By comparison, about 16 percent of middle-class whites were in similar organizations. The highest number of black middle-class joiners belonged to job-related associations or mutual benefit or service groups. Only 10 percent were in church-related groups or political organizations. The highest percentage of white middle-class joiners was also found in job-related associations, but, unlike the finding for blacks, the next most popular choice was church affiliated. Less than half as many whites as blacks belonged to political organizations.

It is clear that the new black middle class was very different from its predecessor in terms of its organizational affiliations. While social clubs had not disappeared altogether, the majority shunned these for less frivolous job- or service-related groups. There is little doubt that in part this changed orientation was a result of the long and often bloody struggles of the civil rights movement. About one-fourth of the new black middle class had either participated directly in civil rights activities or belonged to a civil rights group. Most of the former had been involved in some kind of organized protest, such as a march, demonstration, boycott, or picketing. While some had participated only once, many had done so frequently or at least a few times. Of those belonging to a civil rights group, the majority held membership in the NAACP.

The new black middle class also took seriously its hard-won access to the ballot box, participating in electoral politics at even higher rates than the white middle class. About 81 percent had voted in the 1972 presidential election, compared to 78 percent of middle-class whites. Also, higher percentages of middle-class blacks had voted in state and local elections.

The most impressive change in the life style of the new black middle class was in their social and recreational life. Living now in a desegregated world, they were able to utilize community facilities to an extent undreamed of by the old black middle class. Social life had moved from the home to the community, and organizational membership reflected the serious nature of their interests. As was seen earlier, however, middle-class blacks were still likely to encounter racial slurs, unpleasant incidents, and even discrimination at work and in the community. In moving into the larger society, therefore, they adopted protective practices. There developed a tendency to be selective in the places they frequented, with a preference for those where other blacks were likely to be found.

The search for the good life in the suburbs continued with caution. While some ventured into predominantly white neighborhoods, many others opted for the familiarity and safety of those neighborhoods where other blacks had already settled. The life style of the new black middle class continued to be constrained by racism still active in American society.

# 8

# The New Black Middle Class in the 1980s: Checking Its Vital Signs

The term "vital signs" may imply that the patient is very ill. The black population may not be eligible for intensive care, but it is extremely vulnerable. In 1982, at the nadir of the severest postwar recession the United States has experienced, black unemployment rates soared to a record 18.9 percent, compared to a rate of 8.6 percent among whites. In that same year, the growth of the black middle class *came to a halt* and *even declined*. In 1983, as recovery began and economic indicators again moved upward, white unemployment declined to 8.4 percent, and black unemployment continued to climb—to yet a new record of 19.5 percent. This, indeed, is vulnerability. It calls for a readout of the vital signs of growth rate, income, and living standards and brings us face-to-face once more with the question of the significance of race. Confronting us, too, is the all-important issue of the future of the new black middle class.


## IS THE BLACK MIDDLE CLASS STILL GROWING?

The surprising answer to this question is "Yes." Not surprising is the equally important finding that the black middle class grew at a far slower rate in the 1970s than in the 1960s and continues to lag behind in the 1980s. Between 1960 and 1970, the black middle class doubled in size, achieving a growth rate of 106.8 percent. Between 1970 and 1980, its rate of growth declined to 61.9 percent. Whites experienced just the opposite; their middle class increased faster in the 1970s than in the 1960s. What lay behind these divergent experiences, and what happened to the new black middle class during the early 1980s?

## THE DEMAND SIDE: VULNERABILITY

The rapid growth of the new black middle class in the sixties now appears even more unique in light of the developments of the seventies and eighties. I have already argued that newly enacted civil rights legislation in combination with economic prosperity made this unprecedented growth of the black middle class possible. The rate was especially high during the post-civil rights years of 1964 to 1969, averaging between 7.9 and 12.4 percent annually. The 718,000 black workers joining the ranks of the new black middle class during those years constituted two-thirds of its growth for the entire decade. By comparison, the highest growth years for the middle class in the 1970s and early 1980s—1976 to 1979 and 1984—saw the black middle class increase by only 6.7 to 9.9 percent annually. Had the black middle class developed at the same rate in the 1970s as the 1960s, there would have been almost one million more middle-class blacks in 1980: four and one-half million instead of three and one-half.

### RECESSION AND THE BLACK MIDDLE CLASS

The poor showing in the 1970s and early 1980s was in large part a result of blacks' greater vulnerability to economic slowdowns. Wilson argues that "during the serious recession of the 1970s trained and educated blacks continued to improve their positions vis-á-vis whites in terms of income and occupational advancement."[1] In truth, close examination of the data from the 1973–1975 and 1980–1982 recessions reveals that middle-class blacks not only fared far worse than whites during these periods but they actually *lost ground relative to whites.*

While it is true that during recessions the black labor force in manufacturing, construction, and unskilled service experiences the slowest growth, there is also during these periods a reduction of the growth rate in the white-collar sector. As competition for these scarce white-collar jobs increases, discrimination becomes more intense and blacks' share of available jobs shrinks, thus also decreasing the growth rate of the black middle class. The negative effects of the recession are felt *earlier* and continue *longer* among blacks.

As a consequence of the recession that began at the end of 1973, the black middle-class growth rate fell to a mere 2.3 percent by 1974 and stayed near that level until it ended in 1975. In more concrete terms, this 2.3 percent growth rate represented an addition of only about 53,000 new black middle-class jobs, compared to 275,000 in 1978, after recovery, and 239,000 in 1979. The growth rate of the white middle class, however, *continued to climb* through 1974 and saw a reduction only during the last year of the recession. By 1976 (the year after the recession), it had already resumed its prerecession growth rate. For blacks, this did not occur until about 1978. As a result of this steep reduction in its growth rate, the black middle class increased by only 4.8 percent during the three recession years *combined*, a pace far too slow to narrow the gap.

During the 1980–1982 recession, the black middle class grew by 3.4 percent and the white middle class by

2.9 percent. In 1982, the deepest postwar recession year the United States has experienced, the black middle class actually declined in size, losing about 5,000 jobs. In that same year, the white middle class grew, with almost half a million new jobs being added. Clearly, educated blacks do not get their fair share of jobs in the competition with whites during recessions.

It should be emphasized that to close the gap between the size of the black middle class and the white middle class, the black growth rate must be approximately *two times* that of whites for many years to come. Between 1973 and 1982, for example, the black middle class grew by 51.4 percent compared to 28.7 percent for the white middle class. And yet, the proportion of blacks in all middle-class jobs increased by only 1 percent, from 5.8 to 6.8 percent. During the two recessions, the decline in the growth rate of the black middle class was so steep that their position relative to whites remained about the same or worsened. Educated blacks did not fare well in competition with whites for scarce jobs, and many with college or advanced degrees were not able to find jobs in the middle class. Even in the historically "safe" area of government employment, where middle-class blacks are heavily concentrated, a disproportionate number have lost their jobs during recent years. Race remains significant in the 1970s and 1980s. Had the black middle class grown at the same rate in these decades as during the 1960s, 43 percent of black workers in 1984 would have held middle-class jobs; only 39 percent did so. By comparison, 56 percent of whites were middle class in 1984.

## PATTERNS OF GROWTH

Earlier, I pointed out that the black middle class lagged behind the white middle class not only in total size but in their *distribution* over different strata. Specifically, it was shown that blacks were overrepresented at the lower-middle-class level and underrepresented at the upper. Figure 14 shows the changes that occurred in these distributions between 1973 and 1982.[2] Although blacks won additional jobs in each of the four occupational groups of the middle class, clerical workers accounted for almost 50 percent of the gain. Whites gained

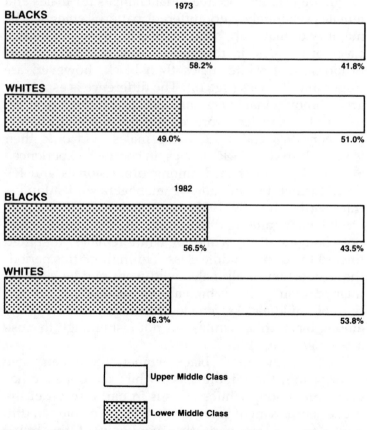

Fig. 14. Changes in the distribution of middle-class blacks and whites, 1973–1982. Source: Handbook of Labor Statistics, December 1983. U.S. Government Printing Office. Washington, D.C.

most in the professional group. In the end, the distribution of middle-class blacks relative to that of whites remained about the same. Overrepresentation in the economically weaker lower middle class has continued into the 1980s.

## Male-Female Differences

When we examine occupational changes for males and females separately, very different patterns emerge. The majority of males are concentrated in the upper middle class; of females, in the lower. A substantially higher proportion of white males than black, however, are upper middle class (fig. 15). The difference is especially great among managers and administrators. And although black males improved their distribution slightly between 1973 and 1982, white males held onto their lead in all strata. Black females, in contrast, experienced a decrease in their lead among professionals and fell even further behind among managers and administrators (fig. 16). By 1982, the relative distribution of black females among different occupational groups had not changed at all, while for white females, it shifted toward the upper middle class. Throughout this period, the proportion of all males who were middle class remained about twice as high among whites. The proportion of middle-class females increased more rapidly among blacks than whites but not fast enough to close a large gap (fig. 17).

Traditionally, more black women than men have made it into the middle class, while the opposite has been true among whites. This is in part a result of the higher employment rates of black women compared to white women; in part, the monopoly of the broad clerical stratum by women; in part, differences in educational attainment (discussed below). An equally impor-

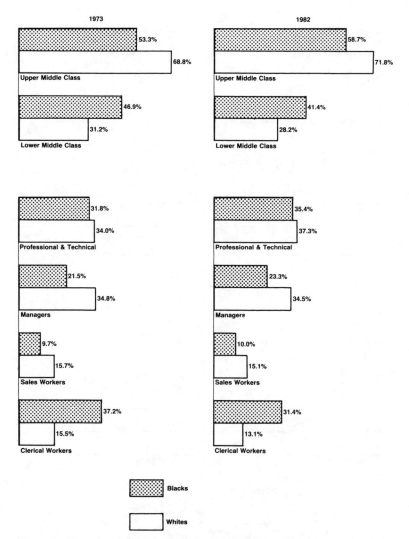

Fig. 15. Changes in the occupational distribution of black and white middle-class males, 1973–1982. Source: Adapted from unpublished tables supplied by the Bureau of Labor Statistics.

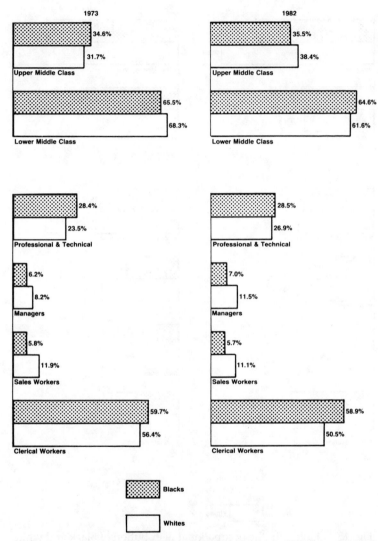

Fig. 16. Changes in the occupational distribution of black and white middle-class females, 1973–1982. Source: Adapted from unpublished tables supplied by the Bureau of Labor Statistics.

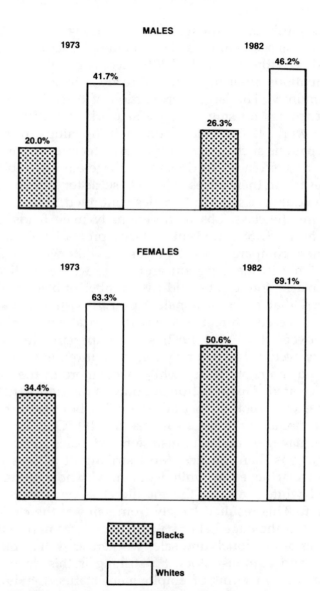

Fig. 17. Changes in the proportion of black and white middle-class males and females, 1973–1982, as percentage of all workers. Source: Adapted from unpublished tables supplied by Bureau of Labor Statistics.

tant contributor to the female edge among middle-class blacks has been patterns of occupational discrimination. Until recently, blacks had little access to middle-class occupations other than those directly serving the black community. The largest proportion of these jobs were in teaching, nursing, and social work—traditional female work. Black males found few openings in male occupations such as accounting, architecture, engineering, and science. And many college-educated black males found themselves obliged to settle for jobs outside the middle class as white males continued to monopolize middle-class jobs in traditionally male fields. As late as 1973, 58.2 percent of black professionals were women, compared to 38.9 percent of white women (fig. 18). Only in management and sales, where relatively few blacks found jobs, did the number of black males exceed that of black females. In 1973, white females outnumbered white males only in clerical work.

Between 1973 and 1982, some important developments occurred which may reflect future trends. First, women, both black and white, won more of the new jobs created. This was true not only in the clerical field, where they took almost all new jobs, but also in the professional and sales areas (see fig. 18). Only among black managers and administrators did males gain more actual jobs than females. Most striking of all was the increase achieved by white women, who now outnumbered white males in the middle class by over three million. This resulted largely from gains at the clerical level, but the edge held by white males was narrowing among professionals and sales workers as well as managers and administrators. So striking is this development that, in terms of employment status, the 1970s might be called the decade of the white female: they entered the work force in record numbers, capturing 63.5 percent of the 12.8 million new white-collar jobs created between 1973 and 1982. Black women also en-

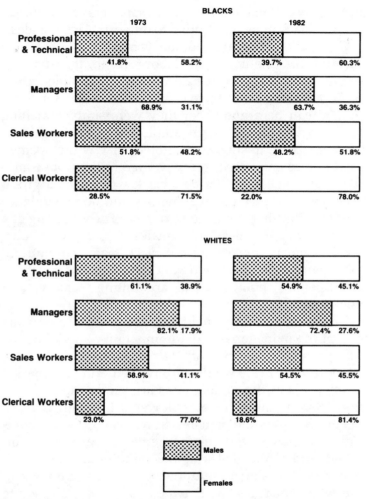

Fig. 18. Percentage of middle-class occupations held by males and females by race and strata in 1973 and 1982. Source: Adapted from unpublished tables supplied by the Bureau of Labor Statistics.

larged their overall lead over black males but primarily
through gains in the clerical field, with only slight gains
in the professional field. Among managers and administrators, black males continued to outstrip black females.

The gains of white women can be attributed to a
record number entering the labor force for the first time
or returning to work during economically troubled times
to supplement their husbands' incomes. To some extent, it can be argued that they were simply catching
up with the already high employment rates of black
women. Still, it should be noted that white women
made more gains than black women at the upper-middle-class level, even though black women as a group
have more labor force experience—additional evidence
of the continuing significance of race. The widening gap
between black males and females at the professional
level suggests, however, that black males continue to
experience difficulty entering occupations not traditionally open to them, such as accounting, science, and
engineering.

The continuing edge held by black women in all strata
except the managerial and administrative should not be
interpreted in matriarchal terms, however. A large
proportion of these women who are entering the market
at all levels of the middle class are single. As a group,
they also continue to earn lower salaries than black
males. Since white females have also gained significantly in closing the employment gap between themselves and white males at the middle-class level, we
may be witnessing a trend toward female dominance in
the white-collar sector. Between 1973 and 1982, white
women increased their proportion of professional jobs
from 38.9 to 45.1 percent. Is the explanation matriarchal
in nature, or is it simply that employers often find it
advantageous to hire females, who in general are paid
lower salaries? Another possibility may be that in the
1970s, the emphasis of affirmative action shifted to

women, away from blacks, and in a tighter economy profited white women more than blacks.

## THE SUPPLY SIDE: MORE VULNERABILITY

Another sobering development in recent years has been the decline in the number of black high school graduates entering college. During the late sixties and early seventies, several factors combined to dramatically increase the number of black students enrolled in college. Principal among these were supportive federal legislation and policies occurring simultaneously with a sharp increase in the population of black youth eligible for college. (Between 1970 and 1980, the college age population of black youth—those 18 to 24 years old—increased by close to one million.) During this period, the federal government either gave black youth access to many formerly all-white colleges or pressured others to increase their black representation. As a consequence of these trends, the percentage of black high school graduates going to college rose from 23.3 percent in 1967 to 26 percent in 1970.[3]

With the exception of a sharp drop in 1973, this trend accelerated steadily in the early 1970s. The proportion of black high school graduates in college reached 33 percent in 1976, equal to whites. Thereafter, the proportion of blacks declined even as the numbers eligible increased. By 1984, the proportion of black college students was down to its 1969 level of 27.2 percent. The enrollment rate of whites after 1976 declined slightly and then rose again, reaching 33.7 percent in 1984. The decline in black college students between 1980 and 1982 occurred in all years of undergraduate training but was especially steep among first-time freshmen enrolling full-time. In 1980, 194,153 black high school graduates enrolled full-time in four-year and two-year colleges and universities. Just two years later, 16,000 fewer new freshmen enrolled even though 216,000 more black high school graduates were eligible. The number of white full-time freshmen also declined between 1980 and 1982 but less sharply (by 3.8 percent, compared to 8.3 percent among blacks). Unlike blacks, however, the decline in white enrollment was matched by a corresponding decrease in the number of high school graduates.

While the number of full-time black students declined in the late 1970s and early 1980s, those enrolled part-time increased. This suggests that the ability of some black families to send their children to college has eroded since the mid-1970s. A large percentage of these are probably working-class families, which have been hardest hit during this period of continued economic decline. Not only have their resources available for education diminished but there are fewer part-time jobs and government grants and loans for students. Since the black middle class has grown primarily through the upward mobility of sons and daughters of skilled and unskilled working-class families, a decrease in their numbers reaching college means a decrease in the supply from this pipeline. These conditions are also certainly hurting the ability of many middle-class black families—especially those in the lower middle class, where the majority is concentrated—to send their children to college.

The number of both full- and part-time black graduate students has also declined in recent years. Those attending school part-time, about two-thirds of all black graduate students, declined by 17.3 percent between 1976 and 1982. The number of full-time black graduate students remained the same from 1972 to 1980, then began declining in the early 1980s. Only black students enrolling for the first time in professional schools, especially in law, medicine, and dentistry, increased during this period. Their numbers grew rapidly between 1970 and 1974, more slowly from 1974 to 1980, then also began declining in the early 1980s. The major cause of this decline is undoubtedly economic. Financial support from schools and opportunities to work have fallen at the same time that the cost of graduate and professional education is rising.

I have already discussed the importance of a college education for mobility into the middle class. Cumulatively, the decline of black students enrolled in college at all levels means that proportionately fewer blacks are able to earn the credentials necessary to enter middle-class jobs, especially those at the upper-middle-class level. The Reagan administration's decision to reduce aid to college students could not have come at a worse time. Given the already negative effect of general economic conditions on the ability of families to afford a college education for their children and the decreased availability of part-time work, today there is a greater need for financial aid from the federal government than ever before.

## THE MALE-FEMALE EDUCATION GAP

In the discussion of the occupational lead held by black women in the middle class, I suggested that in addition to the role played by discrimination against black males in fields not traditionally black, educational differences were a factor. Unfortunately, educational data by sex for college enrollments are not available before 1974. Analysis of these data for 1974 to 1982 reveals overall gains in college enrollments by both black and white females but losses by males. In 1974, the proportion of black females among *full-time* undergraduates exceeded that of black males by 1.4 percent, whereas white females trailed white males by 11.6 percent. Data for full-time *and* part-time undergraduates in 1976 show black female college enrollments 8.4 percent ahead of males, indicating that their lead in education is in part due to higher part-time college attendance. In 1976, enrollment figures for full- and part-time white undergraduates show males ahead, by 5.4 percent. The year 1976 represented the peak for both black and white male college enrollment. Thereafter, their numbers declined, while, except for 1982, the number of females increased. By 1982, the proportion of black female undergraduates had risen to 58.3 percent and that of white females to 51.7 percent.

A similar trend can be observed at the graduate level. Black females increased their numbers among graduate students from 58.7 percent of black graduate students in 1976 to 61.5 percent in 1982; among whites, female graduate students increased from 45.4 to 49.2 percent. Even in professional schools where both black and white males maintained a lead over females, the gap narrowed in the 1970s and early 1980s. Among blacks, women professional students increased from about one-third in 1976 to 44.4 percent in 1982. The percentage of white female professional students nearly doubled, reaching 30.8 percent. These statistics suggest that the occupational gains women made at the middle-class level were in part due to their relative educational gains. In the case of blacks, these educational gains placed women farther ahead in all but professional fields. Among whites, the gains were sufficient to give them a lead at the undergraduate level and near parity among graduate students.

The increasing numbers of females electing to attend college seems to follow the growing emphasis on careers and the need to work. But why the decline in male attendance? Earlier, I pointed out that college-educated females reported having received more economic support than males from their parents. It may be that during a period when families have experienced a relative decline in living standards while the cost of a college education has continued to climb, males have received less and less economic support from their families. With high unemployment, there have also been fewer opportunities to supplement parental assistance with full- or part-time work. The data reveal that the decline in the supply of those with credentials for middle-class jobs is one-sided. Among whites, this has simply brought women to a position of parity with men. Blacks, however, are witnessing a further deterioration of the relative position of males in higher education, with potentially far-reaching consequences for black class structure and family life.

## INCOME: GAINS OR LOSSES?

My analysis of occupational data for the 1970s and 1980s clearly demonstrates that, contrary to Wilson's argument in *The Declining Significance of Race*, educated blacks did not continue to "improve their positions vis-à-vis whites" during recessions as far as occupational achievement is concerned. What about income? Did blacks improve in this area, hold steady, or decline relative to whites? Between 1974 and 1981, the average income of black middle-class males who had year-round, full-time employment increased by 53.5 percent.[4] What at first appears to be impressive progress pales somewhat when compared to an income gain of 68.2 percent among employed white males during this period. As a result of the greater gain of white males, the income gap between black and white middle-class males *widened* rather than narrowed in the 1970s and early 1980s. In 1974, white males, on the average, earned $5,700 more than blacks; in 1981, that gap had opened to $10,042. Income of black males fell behind especially during the recessions of these years. In 1975, the last year of the earlier recession, the black-white male income gap widened from $5,700 to $6,350. In 1980, the gap grew from $6,350 to $8,110 and increased to $10,042 in the second year of that recession. The year 1980 was particularly bad for black income gain: the average income of middle-class black males actually *fell* by 0.3 percent. And it grew by only 1.8 percent in 1981. The average income of white males increased by 7.2 and 8.8 percent in 1980 and 1981, respectively. Because of a complete change in the occupational code by the Census Bureau, it is not possible to compare 1981 income with subsequent years. But, given the severity of the recession in 1982, it is likely that the gap continued to widen in that year.

Blacks fell behind in the 1970s and 1980s even in the professional stratum, where educational credentials are closest to being equal. Between 1974 and 1981, the average income of black professionals increased by only 38.7 percent, compared to 66.7 percent among whites. Again, the result was a widening of the income gap—in this case, from $3,976 in 1974 to $10,418 in 1981. Black middle-class males fell further behind in this period, proving again the vulnerability of the progress made by the black middle class. Black middle-class females, especially those in upper-middle-class occupations, also lost ground at this time, although the income gap was not as great as among males. Between 1974 and 1981, the average income of all black middle-class females rose by 73.9 percent. That of white middle-class females grew by 77 percent, widening their lead from less than $100 in 1974 to $295 in 1981. Most striking of all was the experience of white female professionals, who extended their lead in average income from $544 to $1,017. Only among clerical workers did black females have a higher average income than whites, about $186.

We saw that during this period, white women occupationally gained more at the upper-middle-class level and black women at the lower. The same was true for income, in spite of the fact that as a group black women have more work experience. Comparisons after 1981 using the new occupational codes show a continuation of the trends discussed above. White females continued their slight income edge in all areas except the clerical field. White males widened their already substantial lead in all groups except sales workers, where the gap narrowed slightly.

As a result of the weakening economic position of black males, black females gained more in income relative to males. In the professional stratum, where males and females are most comparable, black females earned 86 percent of the income of their male counterparts in 1981, up from 70 percent in 1974. White females earned 59 percent of the income of white males in 1981, a gain of 2 percent from 1974.


BLACK BUSINESSES STILL STRUGGLING

In chapter 2, I examined the top 100 black businesses identified by *Black Enterprise* to find out if black business in the new black middle class was charting a new course, one different from that of the old service-oriented black businesses. The most hopeful sign in the mid-1970s was the appearance of manufacturing companies that produced goods for the general market. The majority, however, were still service oriented, with little or no appeal to whites. What has happened in the ensuing years, and what can be expected in the future?

On the positive side, total sales of the top 100 black businesses grew from a modest $601.1 million in 1973 to $2.3 billion in 1983.[5] The new leader of the pack, Johnson Publishing, edging out Motown Industries for the first time, earned over $100 million in sales compared to $27.8 million in 1973. Motown Industries also topped $100 million in 1983, with total sales of $108.2 million, up from $46 million in 1973. The number of employees was also up dramatically at Johnson Publishing, from 245 to 1,690. However, there was a decline at Motown from 375 to 231 employees.

These figures represent impressive growth over a ten-year period, yet neither Johnson Publishing nor Motown made the *Fortune* 500 list or even came close. The *last company* on the *Fortune* 500 list, Tandem Computers with sales of $418.3 million, grossed almost four times as much as Johnson Publishing in 1983 and had 4,396 employees.[6] Exxon, which had gross sales of $88.5 billion in 1983 and employed 156,000 people, was number 1 on the list. The top 163 companies on the *Fortune* 500 list each had gross sales exceeding the top 100 black businesses *combined*. This is not to belittle or diminish the success of the *Black Enterprise* top 100 black businesses. They have made significant strides over the past ten years. Within the U.S. economy, however, they are still *small businesses*. Their owners make up part of the petite bourgeoisie rather than an upper class. Nor is there even a possibility that any of these companies will make it into the *Fortune* 500 in the near future, and, therefore, there is no hope for the emergence of enough qualifying individuals to create a black upper class in the foreseeable future.

In 1983, a large percentage of these top 100 companies were still providing services primarily to the black community. Cosmetics, communication and publishing, entertainment, supermarkets, and food services made up about one-fourth of the companies on the list. Automobile dealerships, comprising another one-third, made up the largest single category. The number of black businesses engaged in manufacturing declined over the ten-year period, leaving only twelve in 1983— five of which manufactured cosmetics for black women.

More hopeful was the appearance of a number of

companies in the petroleum sales and high-technology fields. The ten in petroleum sales accounted for 15 percent of the total sales of the one hundred businesses; the five high-technology companies, another 5.7 percent. The number of employees hired by the top black businesses had also risen significantly since 1973—up from 9,499 to 22,098. Still, it is easy to find *individual* companies on the *Fortune* 500 list with as many workers. For example, Gillette, 169 on *Fortune*'s list, had 29,400 employees in 1983 and grossed almost $2.2 billion in sales. Zenith radio, 246 on the list, employed 30,000 workers and earned $1.3 billion. Black businesses have come a long way since the forties and fifties but are still playing in the bush league.

## BACK TO THE BOTTOM LINE: LIVING STANDARDS

Occupational and income gains or losses ultimately set living standards. In the mid-1970s, as we learned earlier, *upper*-middle-class blacks had an average family income sufficient to maintain a middle-class living standard. White upper-middle-class families exceeded that standard, on the average, while lower-middle-class families, both black and white, fell short. Most black families, moreover, needed two full-time incomes to achieve this living standard; most whites managed on one income. In 1976, the economy was just pulling out of a deep recession but carrying blacks along more slowly than whites. Middle-class blacks, in fact, only enjoyed about two years of "full recovery" (1978 and 1979) before being staggered again by an even severer recession from 1980 to 1983. What impact did all of this have on their living standard in the late 1970s and early 1980s?

To answer that question, I compared U.S. Census Bureau family income data with the Bureau of Labor Statistics Family Budgets for the years 1977 to 1981.[7]

These census data differ slightly from my 1976 data in that they include single-parent middle-class families while my own data were confined to two-parent families. The census data are therefore representative of a broader spectrum of the middle class. The difference this makes can be seen from a comparison of average family income in 1976 using the two data sets. The census data average for all middle-class black families was $17,981 in 1976, $3,340 lower than the average for the two-parent families in my sample. The average for white families using census data was $24,550, $1,207 higher than the families in my survey. The higher white average results from the inclusion of all sources of family income in the census data, not just income from salaries and wages.

The BLS higher budget for a middle-class living standard increased by 6.1 percent between 1976 and 1977, to $25,202; the intermediate budget rose to $17,106. The average family income of black middle-class families rose at the slower pace of 4.9 percent; that of whites, by 8.8 percent. The faster growth rate of white middle-class income brought their average to $26,700 in 1977, keeping them above the BLS higher budget. But at $18,864, the average income of middle-class black families fell well below the BLS estimate for a middle-class living standard. It was, in fact, only about $1,700 above the intermediate budget for that year.

Upper-middle-class black families fared better, reaching $21,074 and $22,917 for those in the professional and managerial strata, respectively. However, lower-middle-class clerical families had an average income of only $15,098, below even the BLS intermediate budget. Among whites, only families whose head was a clerical worker had average incomes below the BLS higher budget.

The remainder of this period, to 1981, saw black

families falling further behind. Between 1977 and 1981, the BLS higher budget rose by 60.2 percent to $38,060, while the average income of black middle-class families rose by only 37.4 percent to $25,924—$12,136 lower than the BLS higher budget. In fact, at $25,924, the *average* income of black middle-class families was only equal to the BLS intermediate budget of $25,407 in 1981. Even upper-middle-class black families had average incomes well below the BLS higher budget in 1981.[8] It is probable, then, that only black upper-middle-class families with two earners were keeping up with the increasing cost of maintaining a middle-class living standard.

Between 1977 and 1981, the average family income of white families rose by 42.9 percent. While this was slower than the rise in cost of a middle-class living standard, the slower pace nevertheless left their average of $38,141 in 1981 *equal to* the BLS higher budget. Those in the upper middle class exceeded that budget by several thousand dollars. Part of the difference in the average incomes of middle-class blacks and whites in these comparisons is due to a higher proportion of single-parent families among blacks. The lower income gains of black males and the entrance of more and more white females into the work force are also important contributors to this growing income gap among black and white middle-class families. It should also be recalled that analysis of my 1976 data revealed that it was only by having two full-time earners that upper-middle-class black families have managed to reach and maintain a middle-class living standard. Most of those with only one income and those in the lower middle class have fallen short of this goal. The recessions of the 1970s and 1980s and generally slower economic growth rates among blacks during the post-1960s era have resulted in a significant erosion of living standards among the new black middle class.

## THE POSTRECESSION MIDDLE-CLASS BLUES

The year 1983 demonstrated the uniqueness of the black experience in a paradoxical manner. As the recession came to a halt at the end of 1982 and the United States began what economists were later to call a strong recovery, the total black labor force was enlarged by about 166,000 new jobs and the black middle class resumed its growth. At the same time, black *unemployment continued to rise* to yet a new postwar record of 19.5 percent. How could this happen? The answer seems to lie in the fact that the economy grows unevenly. One sector may grow faster than another or even add new jobs while the other contracts. In this case, the white-collar sector rebounded from the recession more strongly than manufacturing and construction, creating new white-collar jobs faster than blue-collar jobs. A comparison of the total number of new jobs with the growth of the black and white middle classes revealed that most of the new jobs in 1983 were indeed created in the white-collar sector. As the economy continued its recovery in 1984, 42 percent of new jobs entered by black workers and 62 percent of those entered by whites were at the middle-class level. Still, the black unemployment rate remained at 15.9 percent, a percentage point above the high in the 1973–1975 recession. This persistence of high unemployment and sluggish growth at the blue-collar level is an ominous sign that I will return to below.

## FUTURE OF THE NEW BLACK MIDDLE CLASS

It is clear that the future of the black middle class can only be assessed within the context of the future of the U.S. economy. From that point of view, developments in the late 1970s and the 1980s have made it painfully clear that the country now faces economic problems unknown since the Great Depression. An overvalued dollar in the world currency market has made U.S. goods more difficult to sell abroad and foreign goods more attractive to American consumers. Together, these two developments transformed the United States into a debtor nation in trade, with a $140 billion trade deficit that has dampened economic expansion. This weak expansion, in turn, could not lower unemployment rates to their 1950s and 1960s levels. Finally, a federal budget deficit close to $200 billion three years after the 1980–1982 recession which shows no sign of abatement continues to sap energy from the economy.

In this environment, economists make wildly different predictions, from a new recession and higher unemployment rates to growth rates of 4 to 5 percent. Alan Greenspan, of Townsend-Greenspan and Co. and a former chairman of the Council of Economic Advisors, reflected this mood of uncertainty when he wrote in his forecast:

> The potential range of error in any set of economic projections has widened over the past decade. The current environment provides little reason to suppose that those dynamics have been reversed.
>
> Indeed, the number of currently looming problems, many with outcomes conditioned by factors other than the business cycle, stretches the range of economic possibilities to an unprecedented degree. As a consequence, the economy has broken out of any pattern of normal cyclical development.[9]

The message is clear. Economic forecasting, always a difficult task, has become even murkier under present economic conditions. One thing seems certain, however. The above problems are structural and long term, defying any quick fix. It is probably safe to predict continued slower economic growth rates than in the late 1960s. Slow growth translates into a continued but modest increase in the size of the black middle class—at a pace similar to that of the 1970s and early 1980s. Between 1973 and 1981, the black middle class grew by 1.2 million, a 51.6 percent increase. Relative to other classes, this represented an increase of from 28.6 to 37.8 percent of all black workers. At this rate of growth (6.45 annual average), the black middle class will constitute 48.6 percent of all black workers in 1990 and 56.4 percent in the year 2000 (fig. 19). Should the white middle class continue its present growth at the rate of 3.4 percent annually, it will make up 59.5 percent of the white labor force in 1990 and 63 percent in the year 2000. At the present growth rates of these classes and the black and white total labor forces (1.89% for blacks and 2.15% for whites), the black middle class will not have overtaken the white middle class in total size by the year 2000. Further, with present growth trends in the upper- and lower-middle-class strata, blacks will continue to be far more concentrated at the lower-middle-class level than whites—even when they reach parity in total size sometime in the second decade of the twenty-first century. If present trends continue, in the year 2000, less than half of all middle-class blacks (48%) will be in the upper middle class compared to 58 percent of all middle-class whites. It will be far into the twenty-first century before blacks equal the distribution of whites in the upper middle class.

The continued growth of the black middle class during these troubled economic times is in part a result of their sharing in the economy's general trend of faster growth in the white-collar sector than in manufacturing and unskilled service. Between 1960 and 1970, 73.7 percent of the 12.9 million new jobs added to the labor force were at the white-collar level. This share increased to 80 percent between 1973 and 1981. Even in 1961, 1975, and 1982, the nadirs of the three severest postwar recessions, when the total labor force actually shrank, the white-collar sector continued to expand. With the excep-

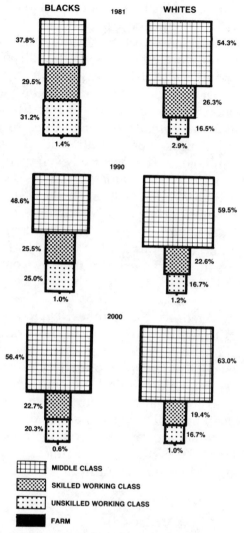

Fig. 19. The black and white class structures in 1981 and projected class structures for 1990 and 2000.

tion of 1982, blacks have always managed to participate somehow in this unbroken expansion of the white-collar sector. The degree to which they shared in this growth depended on the strength of the economy. The slower the growth rate, the smaller the portion of available jobs blacks secure. At the deepest part of the 1980–1982 recession, the black middle class not only did not grow but it shrank in size while the white middle class continued to expand by 483,000 new jobs. Over the entire 1973 to 1981 period, blacks gained only 9.8 percent of the 12.2 million new white-collar or middle-class jobs added, though they constitute 11 percent of the employable adult population—noninstitutionalized civilians 16 years of age and older. This occurred even though about 97 percent of all new jobs gained by blacks during this period were at the white-collar level. Blacks also gained far less than whites at the upper-middle-class level—49 percent compared to 70 percent. In fact, almost half of the new middle-class jobs gained by blacks from 1973 to 1981 were in the clerical stratum. By comparison, whites gained only one-fourth of their new jobs among clericals.

During troubled economic times, even young educated blacks lose out in the competition with whites. Evidence from the late 1970s indicates that sustained growth rates over *several years* of between 5 and 6 percent GNP are required for blacks to get their fair share of middle-class jobs that are being created. Even then, they do not do as well as whites at the upper-middle-class level. Needless to say, the economy has not managed that kind of growth for some time and shows no sign of doing so in the near future.

## THE MIDDLE CLASS VERSUS THE WORKING CLASS AND UNDERCLASS

The size of the middle class can be discussed in both absolute and relative terms. When we note the 1.2 million new jobs added to the black middle class between 1973 and 1981, we are speaking in absolute terms.

Learning that this raised the number of middle-class blacks to 3.5 million provides useful information but fails to give us perspective on the *relative position* of the middle class within the total black class structure. Is it larger, smaller, growing faster, or growing slower than the skilled and unskilled working classes? To answer these questions, we must compare its numbers and growth rate to those of other classes. As an extreme example, the black middle class would not increase in *relative* size if all classes grew at the same rate. Conversely, it could "grow" relative to other classes *without adding numbers* if the numbers in other classes declined. This happened in 1982 when the black middle class increased from 37.8 to 38.4 percent of all black workers even though the *number* of middle-class blacks actually *declined* by some 5,000. This was possible because the other classes combined lost 179,000 jobs.

Historically, the pattern followed within the white class structure has been a steady growth of the middle class with a corresponding decline in the other classes. The big loser in this process has been the farm class, which declined from 28 percent in 1910 to about 3 percent of all white workers by 1980. In the intervening decades, children of farm families—and many adult farmers—moved into the other classes. Some moved up directly into the middle class; others simply replaced workers moving up from the unskilled and skilled strata of the working class. Throughout this period, the *relative sizes* of the white skilled and unskilled working classes remained fairly stable, averaging between 26 and 31 percent for the former and between 13 and 19 percent for the latter. Because of a faster increase in white-collar compared to blue-collar jobs, the white middle class grew from 24 percent in 1910 to 54 percent in 1980 (fig. 20).

This process has not been as smooth among blacks. Unlike whites, black upward mobility into the middle

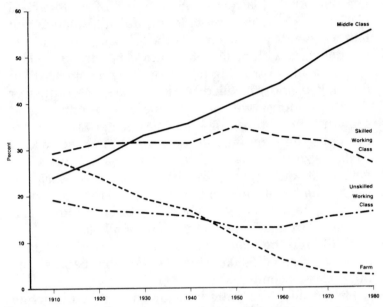

Fig. 20. Changes in the class distribution of the white population, 1910–1980. Sources: Dale Hiestand, *Economic Growth and Employment Opportunities for Minorities* (New York: Columbia University Press, 1964), p. 44; U.S. Bureau of the Census, Census of Population: 1960, U.S. Summary, Detailed Characteristics, table 205; U.S. Bureau of the Census, 1970 Census of the Population, Characteristics of the Population, U.S. Summary, vol. 1, pt. I, sec. 2 (June 1973), table 222, U.S. Department of Labor Statistics, Special Labor Force Report for March 1980.

class progressed at a snail's pace until the late 1960s. Between 1910 and 1940, most blacks moving out of the farm class moved into the unskilled working class, increasing its size from 38.7 percent in 1910 to 47.3 percent in 1940. Between 1940 and 1960, most upwardly mobile blacks moved into the skilled working class, taking jobs primarily as semiskilled operatives. Though declining in relative size after 1940, the unskilled working class remained the *single largest class* among blacks until 1978, when it made up 33.8 percent of all black workers and the middle class 33.6 percent (fig. 21). Since 1978, it has continued to decline slowly, reaching an all-time low of 31.2 percent in 1981. Finally surpassing it, the black middle class grew to 37.8 percent of the black labor force in 1981. Altogether, between 1973 and 1981, the relative size of the black unskilled working class shrank by 5.4 percent, even though the number of unskilled workers remained stable, around 2.9 million. The black skilled working class, while increasing by about 100,000, decreased relatively by 2.6 percent to 29.5 percent of the black labor force.

Unfortunately, not all of this decline in the black skilled and unskilled working classes was the result of upward mobility. In part it was due to the faster increase of middle-class jobs and in part also to an increasing number of unskilled and semiskilled black workers becoming unemployed or unemployed workers dropping out of the labor force altogether (and down into the

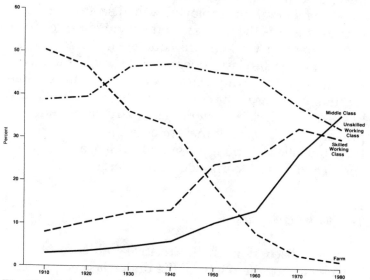

Fig. 21. Changes in the class distribution of the black population, 1910–1980. Sources: See fig. 20.

underclass) because of discouragement. If black workers had the same unemployment rate as whites in 1981, 8.7 instead of 15.6 percent, there would have been approximately 800,000 more employed blacks. It is difficult to calculate exactly how the addition of these workers (and those who dropped out altogether) would affect the size of each class without knowing the class from which they came. Given that the unskilled and skilled working classes experience the highest unemployment rates, it is probably safe to estimate that their addition would increase the size of these classes by 1 to 1.5 percent each and reduce the *relative* size of the middle class correspondingly.

The effects of a sluggish economy on the black class structure, therefore, has been slower absolute growth of the black middle class, higher unemployment, especially within the working class, and a growing group of discouraged workers who have dropped out of the labor force, swelling the underclass. The presence of such a large number of unemployed and discouraged black workers distorts the true size of the various classes since only employed workers are counted in these calculations. The middle class appears a little larger, the skilled and unskilled working classes somewhat smaller than is actually the case. The cumulative effect of these trends has left the black and white class structures differing primarily in the size of their middle classes, the size of their unskilled working class and underclass, and the absence of a black corporate upper class.

### The Black "Underclass"

Wilson's discussion on the relative influence of class versus race on the plight of the underclass emphasizes the impact of the changing economic structure rather than the impact of racial discrimination. He argues that such developments as "the increasing segmentation of the labor market, the relocation of industries out of the central city, and the growing use of industrial technology" are "largely responsible for the creation of a semipermanent underclass in the ghettos."[10] In his conceptual scheme, the underclass is "the very bottom of the economic hierarchy," including "those lower-class workers whose income falls below the poverty level, . . . the more or less permanent welfare recipients, the long-term unemployed, and those who have officially dropped out of the labor market."[11]

Many writers—myself included—would exclude *workers* "whose income falls below the poverty level" from the underclass, preferring to place them within the unskilled working class (or "lower class" as some call them). Given that the majority of welfare recipients are single mothers with dependent children, elderly individuals, and disabled males, it is equally difficult to see how their position in the class structure is tied to market conditions of the type Wilson mentions. Eliminating the working poor and welfare recipients leaves the long-term unemployed and discouraged workers as the only groups whose "permanence" is possibly tied to these economic trends.

But my disagreement with Wilson's analysis is not over the negative effect of these structural factors on the economic position of the black underclass. Earlier in this chapter, I pointed to the anomaly of a resumption of growth in the labor force, including the black middle class after 1982, with continued record high black unemployment. Changing structural conditions do negatively affect the black labor force. My contention, however, is that Wilson underestimates the continuing effect of racial discrimination. Analysis of recent trends indicates that just as educated blacks have not received their fair share of middle-class jobs, so too black workers with limited education and training have not received their fair share of skilled and unskilled working-class jobs because of discrimination. Blacks landed only 2.8 percent of the 3.4 million new blue-collar and unskilled service jobs created between 1973 and 1981; whites, 83 percent.

Between 1973 and 1981, the number of black workers declined by 31 and 37 percent, respectively, among unskilled laborers and domestic workers and grew by only 18.8 percent among unskilled service workers. White unskilled service workers increased by 26 percent. The recent high unemployment rates of blacks, therefore, is in part due to the difficulty of securing sufficient jobs in the unskilled service area to offset losses among laborers and domestic workers. We seem to be witnessing a restructuring of the unskilled working class toward the unskilled service area, such as jobs in hospitals, restaurants, the hotel industry, and protective services. These types of jobs have doubled since 1960 and are now more than twice as numerous as unskilled labor and domestic jobs combined. Though these "new unskilled working-class jobs" do not require much education or training and are primarily located in the central city, blacks are finding themselves increasingly shut out of this work. In the face of a declining skilled working class, white workers are turning to jobs in the unskilled working class and winning out in the competition with blacks, largely because of discrimination. The results are unprecedented high unemployment rates and a growing number of discouraged black workers. Thus, it appears that occupational discrimination continues to be at least as important as economic change in maintaining a large black underclass and a large black unskilled working class. Race remains very significant in the post-1960s, post-civil rights era.

What policies are required to reduce the large size of the black unskilled working class and the growing underclass? Before answering, it is necessary to understand the process whereby the white unskilled working class declined. It declined through opportunities for adult workers to move up into the skilled working class and for better educated unskilled working-class children to seize opportunities in the skilled working and middle classes. Together with the natural attrition of adult workers leaving the labor force through death and retirement, these factors produced a substantial net outflow from the unskilled working class. Over time, more white workers left the unskilled working class than entered it. This net outflow into other classes also kept their unemployment rate down.

While upward mobility of black adult workers and their children into the skilled working and middle classes has occurred, the rate has generally been too slow to result in a net outflow large enough to significantly reduce the size of the black unskilled working class—even after a declining farm population ceased to supply workers to the unskilled working class. Policies likely to reduce the large number of unskilled black workers, therefore, are those that promote upward mobility. This includes policies that stimulate growth of the manufacturing and construction sectors, such as a reduction of our trade imbalance and modest interest rates, which encourage home construction and buying. More skilled and semiskilled working-class jobs will provide opportunities for upward mobility of adult workers and their children into that class. Educational measures to curb the high dropout rate of inner city black youth and economic support to lift sagging college enrollments will provide black youth with the skills needed to compete for jobs in the skilled working and middle classes.

These policies might be sufficient if blacks had an equal chance of winning in the competition for jobs. This has not been and is still not the case. I have shown that blacks continue to lose out in this competition—

even for unskilled service jobs. This is because of persistent discrimination at all levels of the class structure. I have also argued that this discrimination intensified during periods of economic slowdowns. This is clear from the fact that during periods of recovery, white unemployment declines much faster than that of blacks. Vigorous enforcement of equal employment opportunity laws at the unskilled and skilled working-class levels must, therefore, be added to policies that stimulate the economy and improve educational achievement.

## The Black "Upper Class"

I have maintained throughout this study that blacks lack an upper class. In arguing this position, I am following the intellectual traditions of Marx and Weber, who equate an upper class with the owners of the means of production. Included in this group are those families and individuals who own or have controlling shares of the large corporations and banks or have amassed large fortunes through a variety of business enterprises or through inheritance. While there are no clear criteria for determining exactly the boundary of this class, Marx's distinction between the owners of the means of production (large corporations) and the petite bourgeoisie (small entrepreneurs) is helpful. In the latter group we find most small businesses that do not sell stocks but are wholly owned by an individual or partnership. Also included are medium-sized publicly and privately owned firms. Few of these businesses have the capital to reach the size that would eventually put their owners into the ranks of the upper class through large profits from sales. The really successful businesses either started long ago when competition was limited or recently with the aid of large sums of money. Federal

Express, for instance, was started in 1973 by Frederick W. Smith, who had inherited $3.2 million from his father. The business had over $2 billion in revenues in 1984. And his 9.4 percent share is reportedly worth $210 million, enough to win him a place on the *Forbes* list of the four hundred richest persons in the United States.[12]

This list, which *Forbes* compiles yearly, and the *Fortune* 500 list of major corporations are perhaps the two best guides to the upper class. Though arguments might be successfully made for the inclusion of others in the upper class, a more liberal definition than is used by *Forbes* and *Fortune* would not bring many blacks into this select group. I have already pointed out that no black business comes close to winning membership in the *Fortune* 500 list, nor is there any likelihood that any will do so in the near future. Only one black, John Johnson, publisher of *Ebony* and *Jet*, was eligible for the *Forbes* Four Hundred list in 1985. His net worth of about $160 million placed him at the lower end of this list, in which the least wealthy had fortunes around $150 million. The richest person on the list, Sam Moore Walton, owner of Wal-Mart Stores, had a fortune of $2.8 billion in 1984 from a 39 percent share of Wal-Mart.

In a country of billionaires and multimillionaires, a simple millionaire can hardly be included in the upper class. They are rather at the top of the upper middle class. In a country where many individuals can earn $60,000 a year as administrators in government service and dual earner couples can bring home $100,000, the standards for membership in the upper class are steep indeed. More important, we cannot lose sight of the definition of the upper class as owners of the means of production, even as we stretch this to include those who provide services as well as commodities. While a generous definition of the criteria for membership in this class might net a few blacks, there are far too few to constitute a black upper class. Those scholars who have argued for the existence of a black upper class have failed to distinguish between class and status. Blacks do have an upper status group but no upper class.

## 1983 AND BEYOND: CAUTION AND CONCERN REPLACES OPTIMISM

In 1976, middle-class blacks were still optimistic about the future even though echoes of a recent recession had not yet totally disappeared. It had been the "oil embargo recession." Externally induced, it was not seen as a sign of a weakening economy. The even severer recession of 1980–1982 in the absence of any external inducement dashed the optimism felt in 1976 by black and white alike. Instead of 1981 being the year in which they had attained the "best possible life," it brought the drumbeat of deepening economic woes. For blacks, the 1980–1982 recession was especially damaging not merely because of its severity but because they had just barely recovered from the previous one.

In the sobering postrecession climate of the mid-1980s, there is little talk about reaching the best imaginable life in the next five years. Instead, there is concern about the impact on job opportunities of an overvalued dollar and a record $20 billion deficit and concern about interest rates, unemployment, the rate of economic growth, and, especially, fear of a new recession. With economists afraid to make any long-term projections, the future growth of the black middle class remains unclear. It is unlikely that in the near future there will be another period of expansion equal to that of the late 1960s. The ingredients are just not present. Reducing substantially our trade imbalance, which many economists see as the major cause of sluggish economic growth, will take years if it can be done at all. Our economy seems to have entered a qualitatively new phase in which the optimism of the 1960s is replaced by anxiety.

In 1983, the year after the recession, the white middle class grew by 2.8 percent and the black middle class by 2.8 percent—not enough to close the gap. As economic recovery peaked in 1984, growth rates reached 8.4 percent for blacks and 4.1 percent for whites, about the pace needed to keep up with white middle-class expansion and perhaps close the gap a little. But by 1985, the recovery began running out of steam, leaving the economy creeping along once more at a 1 to 2 percent growth rate. In this climate, the best that can be expected is the continued slow growth of the black middle class characteristic of the 1970s; at worst, a new recession and even slower growth.

In this study, I have tried to understand both the emergence of the new black middle class and the living standard of those who have achieved this position. This analysis has demonstrated that we cannot take for granted that blacks who move into the middle class have "made it," have found the American Dream. Not only is the struggle to reach the middle class more difficult for blacks, resulting in fewer getting there, but, once there, middle-class blacks have a more difficult time than whites in maintaining a middle-class living standard. Most of those who manage this standard do so with the assistance of two full-time incomes. Being heavily concentrated in the lower middle class, far more blacks than whites find scant consolation from the label, having to content themselves with living below the accepted standards for their class.

During the 1970s and 1980s, the struggle has become more intense. Relatively fewer blacks are making it into the middle class, and those already there are experiencing an erosion of their already tenuous economic position. While some of the blame can be attributed to a sluggish economy, it is clear also that scarcity has led to an intensification of employment discrimination. As a result, educated blacks are not getting their fair share of available white-collar jobs. At a time when the income gap should be shrinking because of the entrance of more highly educated young blacks into the middle class, the gap has widened even at the professional level. During these times, a renewed emphasis on civil rights legislation is required to safeguard the gains already made and to ensure that blacks will win their fair share of jobs and income. The neglect and even hostility of the Reagan administration toward enforcement of proven affirmative action policies such as quotas and timetables has already caused considerable damage to the process.[13] There is a need for renewed vigilance on the part of blacks and whites alike to ensure continuation of the progress toward a just and fair society that was begun during the civil rights movement. Commitment to and vigorous enforcement of affirmative action laws are needed now more than ever.

The black middle class, as I suggested in the beginning of this study, is a kind of bellwether of black progress. Its very existence gives hope to blacks in other classes, hope that they or at least their children might yet reach the American Dream. But, as we have seen, it is hope tempered by caution and even anxiety. The nagging question, "But how is it up there?" will not go away. And the answer is not reassuring. The economic gap between middle-class blacks and whites remains large and at this time is actually widening. This trend may yet reverse itself and bring on economic conditions that will narrow the gap and even lead to convergence. Signs of such a reversal are not present today, however, and the year 2000 will certainly witness continuing large income and occupational differences.

In the 1960s, unilinear progress and unlimited growth were still the dominant beliefs of the society. Then, it only seemed necessary for blacks to enter this fast lane. If only the detours and roadblocks were removed, blacks would catch up. To push the metaphor a little further, blacks soon found themselves caught up in an economic traffic jam instead. They also discovered in the 1970s and 1980s that many detours and roadblocks remained. Economic equality for blacks, even for the black middle class, now seems a long way off. Uncertainty has replaced enthusiasm and optimism. Even should economic conditions alter sufficiently to bring parity to the middle class, we now know that this does not automatically mean improvement in the economic conditions under which the black unskilled working class and underclass live. The schism in the economy between the white-collar service sector and the blue-collar productive and unskilled service sectors is deep and structural. Growth at the middle-class level no longer implies a corresponding decline in the number of unskilled workers and underclass individuals. The emergence of the black middle class, then, is a hopeful sign in the history of blacks in America. It is not a sign that all is well.

# Notes

*Introduction: Middle-Class Blacks and the American Dream*

1. David M. Katzman, *Before the Ghetto: Black Detroit in the Nineteenth Century* (Chicago: University of Illinois Press, 1973), pp. 121–122.

2. In the discussion that follows, these occupational groups will be referred to as strata within the middle class. Frequently, sales workers and clerical workers will be combined and discussed as one because of their similar position within the middle class. In such cases, I use the term "stratum" rather than the more cumbersome "combined strata." Because of the way data are reported, small businessmen and managers will also be discussed as one stratum at times. With the exception of chapter 8, therefore, the discussion will focus on three principal strata—professionals, managers and small businessmen, and sales and clerical workers—or will divide the middle class into upper middle class (professionals, managers, and small businessmen) and lower middle class (sales and clerical workers).

3. Ralf Dahrendorf, *Class and Class Conflict in Industrial Society* (Stanford: Stanford University Press, 1959), chap. 2. Maurice Zeitlin, "Corporate Ownership and Control: The Large Corporation and the Capitalist Class," *American Journal of Sociology* 79 (March): 1073–1119. Erik O. Wright, "Class

235

Boundaries in Advanced Capitalist Societies," *New Left Review* 98 (July–August): 3–41.

4. The editors of *Fortune, The Changing American Market* (Garden City, N.Y.: Hanover House, 1955). Kurt Mayer, "Recent Changes in the Class Structure of the United States," *Transactions of the Third World Congress of Sociology,* vol. III (1956): 72; "The Changing Shape of the American Class Structure," *Social Research,* vol. 30 (Winter 1963): 468. See also, Mayer, "Diminishing Class Differentials in the United States," *Kyklos,* vol. 12 (1959); and Jessie Bernard, "Class Organization in an Era of Abundance," *Transaction of the Third World Congress of Sociology,* vol. 3 (1956).

5. See John H. Goldthorpe, David Lockwood, Frank Bechhofer, and Jennifer Platt, *The Affluent Worker in the Class Structure* (London: Cambridge University Press, 1973); Gavin Mackenzie, *The Aristocracy of Labor: The Position of Skilled Craftsmen in the American Class Structure* (London: Cambridge University Press, 1973).

6. Evelyn Nakano Glenn and Roslyn Seldberg, "Degraded and Deskilled: The Proletarianization of Clerical Work," *Social Problems,* vol. 25 (1977): 52–64.

*1: The Old Black Middle Class: Dilemma of Race in a Class Society*

1. Louis R. Harlan, ed., *The Booker T. Washington Papers,* vol. 4: 1895–1898 (Chicago: University of Illinois Press, 1975), pp. 22–23.

2. Williard B. Gatewood, "Booker T. Washington and the Ulrich Affair," *The Journal of Negro History,* vol. LV, no. 1 (January 1970): 29–44.

3. Kenneth L. Kusmer, *A Ghetto Takes Shape: Black Cleveland, 1870–1930* (Chicago: University of Illinois Press, 1976), pp. 191–192.

4. Walter B. Weare, *Black Business in the New South: A Social History of the North Carolina Mutual Life Insurance Company* (Urbana: University of Illinois Press, 1973), p. 153.

5. Reynolds Farley, *Growth of the Black Population: A Study of Demographic Trends* (Chicago: Markham, 1970), p. 47.

6. Florette Henri, *Black Migration: Movement North, 1900–1920* (Garden City, N.Y.: Doubleday, 1976), p. 51.

7. William Julius Wilson, *The Declining Significance of Race: Blacks and Changing American Institutions*, 2d ed. (Chicago: University of Chicago Press, 1980).

8. E. Franklin Frazier, *The Negro in the United States*, rev. ed. (New York: Macmillan, 1957), pp. 273–275.

9. W. E. B. Du Bois, *The Philadelphia Negro: A Social Study* (New York: Schocken Books, 1967 [first published, 1899]), pp. 32–36.

10. W. Lloyd Warner and Paul S. Lunt, *The Social Life of a Modern Community* (New Haven: Yale University Press, 1941).

11. See Allison Davis, Burleigh B. Gardner, and Mary R. Gardner, *Deep South*, abridged ed. (Chicago: University of Chicago Press, 1965); St. Clair Drake and Horace R. Cayton, *Black Metropolis: A Study of Negro Life in a Northern City*, vols. I and II (New York: Harper & Row, 1945).

12. See Gunther Roth and Claus Wittich, eds, *Max Weber: Economy and Society* (New York: Bedminster Press, 1968), pp. 302–307, 926–940.

13. Kusmer, *A Ghetto Takes Shape*, p. 93, footnote.

14. Drake and Cayton, *Black Metropolis*, vol. II, pt. IV, p. xxv.

15. Frazier, *The Negro Family in the United States*, rev. and abridged ed. (Chicago: University of Chicago Press, 1957), see n. 8, [1939] p. 317.

16. Frazier, *The Negro in the United States*, p. 279.

17. Frazier, *The Negro Family in the United States*, p. 198.

18. Katzman, *Before the Ghetto*, p. 128.

19. Kusmer, *A Ghetto Takes Shape*, p. 70.

20. James Weldon Johnson, *Along This Way* (New York: Viking Press, 1968 [1933]), p. 41.

21. Katzman, *Before the Ghetto*, p. 106.

22. Cited in Frazier, *The Negro Family in the United States*, p. 297.

23. Kusmer, *A Ghetto Takes Shape*, p. 98.

24. Frazier, *The Negro Family in the United States*, pp. 310–311.

25. Katzman, *Before the Ghetto*, p. 139.

26. Frazier, *The Negro Family in the United States*, p. 308.

27. Cited in Kusmer, *A Ghetto Takes Shape*, p. 106.

28. Frazier, *The Negro Family in the United States*, pp. 320–321.

29. Ibid., p. 321.

30. E. Franklin Frazier, "Occupational Classes Among Negroes in Cities," *American Journal of Sociology*, vol. 35 (March 1930), p. 726.

31. Allan H. Spear, *Black Chicago: The Making of a Negro Ghetto: 1890–1920* (Chicago: The University of Chicago Press, 1967), p. 29.

32. Katzman, *Before the Ghetto*, p. 107.

33. Cited in ibid.

34. Frazier, *The Negro Family in the United States*, p. 317.

35. E. Franklin Frazier, "Durham: Capital of the Black Middle Class," pp. 333–340, in A. Locke, ed., *The New Negro* (New York: Atheneum, 1968). (Originally published by Albert and Charles Boni in 1925.)

36. Drake and Cayton, *Black Metropolis*, p. 438.

37. Joseph A. Pierce, *Negro Business and Business Education* (New York: Harper and Brothers, 1947), pp. 193–194.

38. Abram L. Harris, *The Negro as Capitalist* (Philadelphia: The American Academy of Political and Social Sciences, 1936), p. 54.

39. Kusmer, *A Ghetto Takes Shape*, p. 192.

40. Drake and Cayton, *Black Metropolis*, p. 46.

41. Frazier, "Durham: Capital of the Black Middle Class," p. 339.

42. Carter G. Woodson, *The Negro Professional Man and the Community* (New York: Negro Universities Press, 1934).

43. This section draws on Frazier's excellent review of black higher education in *The Negro in the United States*.

44. Woodson, pp. 32–33.

45. Ibid., p. 33.

46. Ibid., p. 32.

47. Frazier, *The Negro in the United States*, pp. 295–297.

48. Drake and Cayton, *Black Metropolis*, vol. I, pp. 228–229.

49. Peter M. Blau and Otis Dudley Duncan, *The American Occupational Structure* (New York: Free Press, 1967).

50. Drake and Cayton, *Black Metropolis*, p. 759.

51. Ibid., p. 107.

52. Ibid., p. 533ff.

53. Ibid., p. 532.

54. E. Franklin Frazier, *Black Bourgeoisie* (New York: Free Press, 1962 [1957]).

55. Frazier, *The Negro in the United States*, p. 288.

56. Drake and Cayton, *Black Metropolis*, pp. 540–541.

## 2: The New Black Middle Class: Has Race Been Eclipsed?

1. Otis Dudley Duncan, "Patterns of Occupational Mobility among Negro Men," *Demography* 5, no. 1 (1968): 11.

2. Drake and Cayton, *Black Metropolis*, vol. I, pp. xlvi–vii.

3. The editors of *Fortune, The Changing American Market.*

4. Mayer, "Recent Changes in the Class Structure of the United States," p. 72.

5. Mayer, "The Changing Shape of the American Class Structure," p. 468. See also, Mayer, "Diminishing Class Differentials in the United States," and Bernard, "Class Organization in an Era of Abundance."

6. C. Wright Mills, *White Collar* (New York: Oxford University Press, 1951).

7. G. Williams Domhoff, *Who Rules America?* (Englewood Cliffs, N.J.: Prentice-Hall, 1967).

8. John Kenneth Galbraith, *The New Industrial State* (Boston: Houghton Mifflin, 1967).

9. E. Franklin Frazier, *Black Bourgeoisie*, p. 188.

10. Drake and Cayton, *Black Metropolis*, vol. II, p. xxiii.

11. See William Graham Sumner, *Folkways: A Study of the Sociological Importance of Usages, Manners, Customs, Mores, and Morals* (Boston: Ginn and Co., 1940), pp. 77–78.

12. Otis Dudley Duncan, "Patterns of Occupational Mobility among Negro Men," p. 19.

13. Wilson, *The Declining Significance of Race.*

14. Ibid., p. 120.

15. Ibid., p. 150.

16. Ibid., p. 121.

17. Ibid., p. 151. Wilson's definition of underclass seems to include those unskilled workers whose income places them below the poverty level.

18. Ibid. Emphasis added.

## 3: Moving On Up: At Last a Piece of the Pie

1. See especially Blau and Duncan, *The American Occupational Structure*, chap. 5.

2. In one analysis using the same model with national representative samples of young males aged 14–24 in 1966, the $R^2$ (a measure of the amount of the outcome explained) for occupational attainment in 1966 was .446 for white males but only .293 for black males.

3. Herbert Gutman, *The Black Family in Slavery and Freedom* (New York: Random House, 1976); Frank F. Furstenberg, Jr., Theodore Hershberg, and John Modell, "The Origins of the Female-Headed Black Family: The Impact of the Urban Experience," *The Journal of Interdisciplinary History* 6 (1975): 211–233; P. J. Lammermeier, "Urban Black Family of the Nineteenth Century: A Study of Black Family Structures in the Ohio Valley, 1850–1880," *Journal of Marriage and the Family*, vol. 35 (August 1973): 440–456.

4. Elmer P. Martin and Joanne Mitchell Martin, *The Black Extended Family* (Chicago: University of Chicago Press, 1978).

5. See the introduction for a description of this sample.

6. See Blau and Duncan, *The American Occupational Structure*, chap. 5, for an excellent explanation of the technique. Briefly, path analysis is a multiple regression technique allowing the calculation of both direct and indirect effects. Thus, the direct influence of a father's education on his son's education as well as the indirect effect of a father's education on his son's occupation *acting through the son's* education can be measured. The other causal factors included in the analysis were (1) whether or not the mother worked, (2) the number of children, (3) birth order, (4) whether or not both parents

were present, (5) the size of the place where the respondent grew up, (6) the region where the respondent grew up, (7) age of respondent, (8) whether or not respondent's father suggested a particular job, (9) whether or not respondent's mother suggested a particular job, and (10) whether or not others took special interest in respondent when growing up.

7. See Jerold Heiss, *The Case of the Black Family: A Sociological Inquiry* (New York: Columbia University Press, 1975), chap. 7, for a review of relevant research.

8. Otis Dudley Duncan, "Inheritance of Poverty or Inheritance of Race?" pp. 85–110, in Daniel P. Moynihan, ed., *On Understanding Poverty* (New York: Basic Books, 1968).

9. Robert P. Althauser and Sydney S. Spivack, *The Unequal Elites* (New York: John Wiley & Sons, 1975).

10. Ibid., pp. 118ff.

11. Among black males, the betas for the effect of education on first and current (1976) jobs were .361 and .406, respectively. Among whites, the betas for the effect of education on first and current jobs were .378 and .373.

12. Juan Williams, "The Black Elite: Why the Ranks of Washington's Well-Off and Powerful Blacks are Swelling," *Washington Post Magazine*, January 4, 1981, p. 12.

13. Ibid., p. 12.

14. Jacqueline Trescott, "The New Insensitivity: The Veiled Insult and the Direct Slur—Return." *Washington Post*, June 2, 1981, pp. B1–B3.

15. Ibid., p. B3.

16. Ibid., p. B1.

4: *How Big a Piece?*

1. "The Top 100," *Black Enterprise*, vol. 7, no. 11 (June 1977): 63–71.

2. In this analysis, age represents lifetime work experience and time on the job represents seniority. While conceptually distinct, these two factors are in fact correlated (.65 among blacks and .58 among whites), so that when both are

included in the same model, the effect of each is in part masked. To measure the effect of each more accurately, three models were estimated, one with age alone, one with time on the job alone, and a third with both included.

3. In this study, the Nam Occupational Scale was used. See Charles B. Nam and Mary G. Powers, "Changes in the Relative Status Level of Workers in the United States, 1950–60," *Social Forces* 47 (December 1968): 158–170; and Charles B. Nam, John LaRocque, Mary Powers, and Joan Holmberg, "Occupational Status Scores: Stability and Change," *Proceedings of the American Statistical Association,* 1975, pp. 570–575. The Nam scale correlates with the Duncan SEI scale at about .95.

4. See Duncan, "Inheritance of Poverty or Inheritance of Race?" pp. 85–100.

5. For this comparison, regression Model 1 with age was used. An examination of Model 3 reveals that age (work experience) has greater impact on income for black males than does seniority. Model 1 also has a higher $R^2$ than Model 2 with seniority instead of age.

*5: Life in the Middle: In Pursuit of the American Dream*

1. See U.S. Department of Labor, "Three Standards of Living for an Urban Family of Four Persons, Spring 1967" (Springfield, Va.: National Technical Information Service, 1969), p. 1.

2. It was further assumed that the husband aged 38 worked full-time, that the wife did not work, and that the two children were a 13-year-old boy and an 8-year-old girl. While it is obvious that many families, perhaps even the majority, do not fit this pattern, the budgets are useful approximations.

3. See Paul Blumberg's *Inequality in an Age of Decline* (New York: Oxford University Press, 1980) for a sobering assessment of changing economic conditions in the United States.

4. Bureau of Labor Statistics, "Autumn 1977 Urban Fam-

ily Budgets and Comparative Indexes for Selected Urban Areas," *News* (Washington, D.C.: Bureau of Labor Statistics).

5. Bart Landry and Margaret Platt Jendrek, "The Employment of Wives in Middle-Class Black Families," *Journal of Marriage and the Family* (November 1978): 787–797.

6. Thorstein Veblen, *The Theory of the Leisure Class* (New York: Viking Press, 1931).

## 7: Life Style: And the Living Is Easy, or Is It?

1. See *Ebony*'s August 1973 special issue on the black middle class.

2. Sydney Kronus, *The Black Middle Class* (Columbus, Ohio: Charles E. Merrill, 1971); William A. Samson and Vera Milan, "The Intraracial Attitudes of the Black Middle Class: Have They Changed?" *Social Problems*, vol. 23, no. 2 (December 1975): 153–165.

3. John Fine, Norval D. Glenn, and J. Kenneth Monts, "The Residential Segregation of Occupational Groups in Central Cities and Suburbs," *Demography* 8 (February 1971): 91–101.

4. Stanley Lieberson, *Ethnic Patterns in American Cities* (New York: Free Press of Glencoe, 1963).

5. See Karl E. Taeuber, "Racial Segregation: The Persisting Dilemma," *The Annals* 422 (November 1975): 87–96; Leo F. Schnore et al., "Black Suburbanization, 1930–1970," pp. 69–94, in Barry Schwartz, ed., *The Changing Face of the Suburbs* (Chicago: University of Chicago Press, 1976); Daphne Spain and Larry H. Long, *Black Movers to the Suburbs: Are They Moving to Predominantly White Neighborhoods?* U.S. Bureau of the Census, 1981. Special Demographic Analyses, CDS-80-4. Washington, D.C.: U.S. Government Printing Office.

6. The "ring" of an SMSA is that part which is outside of the central city. While the rings of SMSAs contain varying amounts of rural areas, they come close to the definition of a suburb as an urban area outside the large central city. Though most researchers studying suburbs utilize data on

the rings of SMSAs, some use the segment of urbanized areas outside of central cities. The latter is probably a more accurate unit of analysis, as it minimizes the problem of rural areas mentioned above.

7. Reynolds Farley, "Components of Suburban Population Growth," in Barry Schwartz, ed. *The Changing Face of the Suburbs*, p. 9.

8. Larry Long and Diana DeAre, "The Suburbanization of Blacks, *American Demographics* (September 1981): 16–22. The 14 largest cities, each with 200,000 or more blacks in 1980, included New York City, Chicago, Detroit, Philadelphia, Los Angeles, Washington, D.C., Houston, Baltimore, New Orleans, Memphis, Atlanta, Dallas, Cleveland, and St. Louis.

9. Spain and Long, *Black Movers to the Suburbs*, pp. 7–11.

10. Long and DeAre, "The Suburbanization of Blacks," p. 21.

11. Taeuber, "Racial Segregation: The Persisting Dilemma"; Brian J. Berry and John D. Dasarda, "The Congruence of Social and Spatial Structure: Neighborhood Status and White Resistance to Residential Integration as an Example," chap. 2, in *Contemporary Urban Ecology* (New York: Macmillan, 1977).

12. Harold X. Connolly, "Black Movement into the Suburbs: Suburbs Doubling Their Black Population during the 1960s," *Urban Affairs Quarterly* 9 (September 1973): 91–111; Farley, "The Changing Distribution of Negroes within Metropolitan Areas," *American Journal of Sociology* vol. 75 (January 1970) 512–29. Exceptions have existed where blacks moved into newer expanding integrated neighborhoods during the 1960s. In the 1970s, this trend has accelerated among upper-middle-class blacks.

13. Taeuber, "Racial Segregation: The Persisting Dilemma," p. 95.

14. "Leading Black Neighborhoods," *Black Enterprise* (December 1974): 25–33, 61.

15. This index has been called AIC, or "asymmetric intergroup contact," by Brigitte Mach Erbe, in "Race and Socioeconomic Segregation," *American Sociological Review* 40 (December 1975): 801–812, and differs from the more widely used ID (index of dissimilarity) in that it adjusts for the varying

proportions of the relevant groups in the units of analysis. The ID is insensitive to differences in the relative size of subpopulations. Thus, as Erbe demonstrates, it is possible to get the same ID value in cases where the sizes of subpopulations differ radically. By adjusting for these differences in size of subpopulations, the AIC index yields values that reflect these compositional differences.

16. Annemette Sorensen, Karl E. Taeuber, and Leslie J. Hollingsworth, Jr., "Indexes of Racial Residential Segregation for 109 Cities in the United States, 1940–1970," *Sociological Focus* 8 (April 1975): 125–142; Thomas L. Van Valey, Wade Clark Roof, and Jerome E. Wilcox, "Trends in Residential Segregation: 1960–1970, "*American Journal of Sociology* 82 (January 1977): 826–844.

17. Farley, "Components of Suburban Population Growth," pp. 29–31, reports similar findings for Detroit in 1970.

18. Drake and Cayton, *Black Metropolis*, pp. 533ff.

19. Ibid.


*8: The New Black Middle Class in the 1980s: Checking Its Vital Signs*

1. Wilson, *The Declining Significance of Race*, p. 175.

2. These dates were chosen because 1972 is the first year in which the Census Bureau began collecting data for blacks alone. Prior to 1972, all nonwhites were combined. The year 1982 is the last year for which occupational data using the old classification is available.

3. Data for this section come from unpublished reports from the National Center for Education Statistics, the Office for Civil Rights, and the U.S. Census Bureau. See also, Susan T. Hill, "Participation of Black Students in Higher Education: A Statistical Profile from 1970–71 to 1980–81," Special Report (National Center for Education Statistics, U.S. Department of Education).

4. Income data for males and females come from unpublished tables supplied to me by the Bureau of Labor Statistics.

5. See *Black Enterprise*, June 1974 and June 1984.

6. See *Fortune*, April 29, 1985.

7. Data for 1977 through 1979 come from published reports of the Bureau of the Census, Money Income in 1976 of Families and Persons in the United States, Current Population Reports/Consumer Income, U.S. Department of Commerce, 1976, P-60, no. 114, table 36; 1977, P-60, no. 118, table 36; 1978, P-60, no. 123, table 39; 1979, P-60, no. 129, table 41. Data for 1980 and 1981 come from unpublished tables supplied to me by the Bureau of the Census. These data are compiled by the occupation held longest by the family head. One set of tables are for all families, including those heads who worked only part of the year, part-time, or were unemployed. The other tables include only those whose heads worked year-round, full-time. I have used only the latter group for both black and white families since they are more comparable to my own 1976 data.

8. It is true that BLS budgets assume a family size of four and that many of the single-parent black middle-class families included in the census data were smaller. Some of these, therefore, managed to keep up with rising living costs. It should also be recalled that most single-parent families are headed by women, who generally earn lower incomes than their male counterparts.

9. *Washington Post*, September 15, 1985, p. C10.

10. Wilson, *The Declining Significance of Race*, pp. 171, 166.

11. Ibid., p. 156.

12. *Forbes 400* Special Issue, October 28, 1985.

13. The recent decision by the Supreme Court upholding the use of timetables as a remedy for past discrimination is a welcome move.

# Index

Designer: U.C. Press Staff
Compositor: Prestige Typography
Text: 11/13 Palatino
Display: Palatino
Printer: The Murray Printing Company
Binder: The Murray Printing Company